Do You See What I See?

DO YOU SEE WHAT I SEE?

A Devotional of
Inspiring Stories,
Scriptures, Challenges,
and Prayers
for Educators

NORMAN NILES

HARRIS
Author Services

Dedication

To my son, Joshua.

Contents

Semester I: Weeks 1 - 20

Semester II: Weeks 21 - 40

About the Author

Norman N. A. Niles is an award-winning teacher, storyteller, motivational speaker, mentor, husband, father and a child of God. He holds a master's degree in Mathematics from Villanova University, along with a bachelor's degree in Mathematics and a minor in Education from Morehouse College. His experience in the classroom spans two continents and the Caribbean - teaching for eight years in the United States, five years Jamaica, and one in Australia. He has served in schools as chaplain; director of creative arts; department chair; instructor of pedagogy; basketball, track, and golf coach; sports broadcast announcer; and honor society adviser.

Norman likes to play most sports including cross-country running, basketball, and American football. His favorite sport, however, is golf. (His wife, Sarah, loves to shop so the timing works out wonderfully.) He also enjoys spending time with his family, traveling, being outdoors, and telling dad jokes.

In 2018, Norman and his family moved to Australia. While taking a year away from the classroom to be a full-time father to his son, Joshua, Norman was inspired to write this book for educators. As a new parent, he more fully realized how difficult it can be to balance all that life requires. This book encouraged and challenged him as he wrote it and he hopes it does the same for you.

Norman enjoys working with and inspiring youth and adults to find God's solutions to life's problems. His life's motto is Respice Finem - "Keep the End in View," and he believes that, if we pay close enough attention, we can see God working in every aspect of our lives.

Acknowledgements

To my wife, Sarah, for encouraging me throughout this process.

To my sister, Marnel, for always finding the time to help me.

To my brother, Dwan, for his contagious spirit of adventure.

To my mom, Marcia, for her prayers and always checking in on her youngest child.

To my dad, William, for inspiring me more than he can imagine.

Thank you.

Introduction

This book has been written with the hard-working Christian educator in mind. The weekly devotions are written to help you get through each week of school with Christ on your mind and in your heart, whether your school year begins in August, September, or January. Each day should take about five minutes to go through, and hopefully you're able to reflect afterwards or during break times.

The general outline is as follows

Monday	Devotional and Memory Verse
Tuesday	Challenge and Teaching Tip
Wednesday	Time in the Word
Thursday	Prayer
Friday	Your Written Reflection

Mondays set the theme for the week with a memory verse and a devotional thought based on a Bible passage. When was the last time you took the time to memorize a Bible verse? Hopefully it was recently, but if not, here's your chance. I've chosen verses that coincide with the message of the week and I hope you're able to write them down on a sticky note or have this book open to see the verse throughout the week. Between classes, test yourself to see if you've got it down. It is my hope that you're able to commit it to memory by Friday.

On Tuesdays there is a Challenge issued that will test you spiritually, which I trust can be completed (at least in part) by Friday. There is also a pragmatic Teaching Tip that I hope is useful in your day-to-day classroom duties.

Wednesday is the day we take the time to read the Word. More powerful than anything I can write is the Word of God. Please make sure you read the passages prayerfully, as the Word is living and powerful. For easier access, a QR Code has been provided for each of these passages.

Each Thursday there is a prayer that has been written for you. You may choose to pray the prayer or simply read what has been prayed on your behalf. Isn't it amazing that our God answers prayers that people we haven't met have prayed for us? I know that God will do what He's promised and I'm honored to be able to intercede in this way.

Friday is exam day! Did you successfully complete the challenge of the week? Were you able to memorize the Scripture? I've left space for you to reflect on your week and how wonderful or difficult it has been. Please take a few minutes to engage in this written reflection. There is catharsis in writing and, even more importantly, you'll be able to track your progression (just as we love to do with our students).

Feel free to read the days in any order. If one day you need a prayer, check Thursday. If you feel the need to spend time in the Word, be sure to read Tuesday's or Wednesday's section. You can even choose to read the week through at one sitting. It's completely up to you!

I truly hope and pray that this book is a blessing to you and that your students, colleagues, and family are simultaneously able to see more of Christ in you as a result. May God bless you and His ministry of educating His children through you.

Dead Man Talking

Memory Verse - "Pray without ceasing."
1 Thessalonians 5:17

will NOT wash the dishes!"

My hand slammed against the table as my teenage voice loudly uttered this response to my dad's command. Never looking at him directly, I fixed my gaze squarely at my brother who sat across from me. I knew it was a tricky proposition but I was prepared. (I had planned this for at least a day and I knew I had just a few moments before my dad could get around the table to wring my neck.) My brother, in the meantime, was frozen as I'm sure he thought, "I'm going to miss Norman. We had a few good years together..."

After my designed pregnant pause of three or four seconds, I finished my sentence as vociferously as I'd begun it: "...later, I will wash them RIGHT NOW!!" Still refusing to allow my eyes to connect with my dad's, I stormed towards the sink and began cleaning every dish I could find. My brother and I laugh about it to this day. (Years later he tried to bribe his daughter to do the same thing with her mom but she refused, saying money is useless if you're no longer alive.)

As you prepare for a new year with new goals, projects, students, parents, and colleagues, it is my belief that nothing gets you ready better than good preparation. Jesus knew this, of course, as He spent countless hours in prayer during His few years on earth. In the early hours of the morning, He knew His strength for the day lay completely in the hands of His heavenly Father. The closer He got to Calvary, the closer He got to His death, the more fervent His prayers became. This dead Man found the fortitude to keep going in talking to His Dad.

The strength you'll need this year, one day at a time, won't come from properly planned lessons or using the newest pedagogical tactics. Your power comes from heaven. Yes, you must prepare for students and parents who undoubtedly will have seemingly missed some etiquette classes. Yet, with the power of the Holy Spirit preparing you for the trials, you can successfully achieve your goals. Talk with Him consistantly and you'll find that your light for Him will shine more brightly than scrubbed china.

Tuesday - Your Challenge and a Teaching Tip

Challenge: Spend extra time this week in prayer. When you have a break or before you start planning your lessons and decorating your classroom, take time to pray for the students who will sit in those seats and their families. Pray for the employees of the school - from the custodians to the board members. If you can, walk the campus and surround the school in prayer.

Teaching Tip: Always have more planned for a lesson than required, especially early on in the school year. Be prepared for students who may be advanced and, as far as possible, have alternate activities available so that they stay engaged and not become disruptive.

Wednesday - Time in the Word

Matthew 6:5-15

Thursday - Prayer

Lord, more essential than any other type of preparatory work is this time that we spend with You. You tell us to pray without ceasing. Every breath we breathe, every word we speak, every intonation of our voice, every step we take needs to be in tune with You. You've called us to a nearly impossible task - educating students in the 21st century. But You are the God of the impossible. One day at a time, allow us to make a difference in the lives of Your students, leading them not only to earthly knowledge and success, but to an eternal, intimate knowledge of the Eternal One. Give us the strength to stay on our knees so that we might withstand the temptations of the enemy. This we pray in the mighty name of Jesus. Amen.

Friday - Reflection

How was your week? Did you complete the challenge? What lessons did you learn? What did you see God do this week?

_____

_____

_____

Do You See What I See?

_____

_____

_____

_____

Week 2

Be an Ass

Memory Verse - "Let your light so shine before men, that they may see your good works and glorify your Father in heaven."
Matthew 5:16

I should have been meaner.

It went well for the first few periods of my first day teaching and I, being a positive person, thought word had gotten out that students would have to deal with a pretty tough Math teacher. I knew that students tend to take kindness for weakness so I tried to be a little firmer than usual. Unfortunately, I went a little softer during my last class, which somehow ended up being the worst behaved class I had all year long. Who woulda thunk it?

If today is your first day of teaching, let me first say, "Welcome and Congratulations! Please be an ass today."

If you're a seasoned veteran, I'll tell you the same - be an ass today! My auto-correct tried to change *ass* to *asset*, which is something you should be as well, but today and throughout this week my challenge to you is to be an ass.

Let me explain. It's true that students tend to take kindness for weakness and that you probably should be a bit more stern than you usu-

5

ally tend to be when they have just come back from break, but that's not the type of "ass" of which I'm speaking.

Jesus told his disciples before His triumphant entry into Jerusalem that they needed to go out and find an ass on which no one had sat. This would be the animal on which He, the King of Kings and Lord of Lords, would ride. This would be the creature that would *lift up Jesus for all to see*. This would be the animal that trained and worked all its life for this moment. This ass would carry Jesus and go only where and when the Master wanted.

My best advice to you - be an ass today. As students return to classes, be reminded that, no matter how important your subject may be, no matter how wonderful or terrible the students are, the ultimate success in education is our students seeing Christ in us and choosing to follow Him.

Tuesday - Your Challenge and a Teaching Tip

Challenge: Whether you're able to do so publicly or privately in your heart, lift up Jesus this week. Let your attitude and response to situations be such that others know that the Holy Spirit is in you. Take a deep breath when the challenges come (and they will, if they haven't already) and ask God to help you through it. Simply put, you actually want someone to think you're an ass this week - the type that uplifts Jesus!

Teaching Tip: Be firmer than usual today, especially if it's your first day teaching. Be loving, but make sure the students know that there are rules and order in your classroom. Fewer and easy-to-remember rules are usually best.

Wednesday - Time in the Word

Matthew 21:1-11

Thursday - Prayer

Lord, we take this opportunity to thank You for allowing us to work for You. Before us today and this week are students whose stories are all different and we cannot know them all, but You do. Because of that, we place ourselves in Your hand of wisdom and power. We want to balance justice and mercy, as You do. We need, even more than that, to establish You in our hearts that we might do good and have Your name glorified. So please give us what we need each day this week. Allow us to be firm when we need to be, and merciful when we need to be. Ultimately, we pray that You are the One who is seen and heard through all of our interactions. This is our prayer, in Jesus' name. Amen.

Friday - Reflection

How was your week? Did you complete the challenge? What lessons did you learn? What did you see God do this week?

_____

_____

_____

Do You See What I See?

_____

_____

_____

_____

F is for Failure

Memory Verse - "Let us therefore come boldly to the throne of grace, that we may obtain mercy and find grace to help in time of need."
Hebrews 4:16

Forty six! I got a 46 on an exam. In graduate school. On a take-home exam. The scores were so low on the exam that one student had the strength (or audacity) to raise his hand and ask our professor, "What is this graded out of?" It was a hopeful question. All hope was lost when our professor replied in her calm, caring voice, "It's out of 100%."

I'm not sure if you've ever tried your best and completely failed. I was teaching at the time and I thought to myself, "How can I continue to teach Math if I can't pass a Math test?" I was further humbled when the professor whispered in my ear, "You may want to try it again." Let me be clear. It was a take-home test - I hadn't run out of time. I had run out of information in my head.

I realized what I needed to do. It was what I had told my students to do time and time again - get some assistance. From the beginning of the course, I had tried to do everything on my own and now I was drowning. I needed to get some help...and soon!

Peter was in the same boat, maybe figuratively and literally. He had been walking on water toward Jesus when his focus changed and he saw the storm. Immediately he started to drown. He needed help in the worst way. Peter then uttered one of the shortest prayers ever, "Lord, save me!" Just as immediately as he had begun to drown, Jesus' hand reached his and he was safe.

Sometimes you're going to need help. Don't hesitate! If you find yourself having done all you can and yet the storm is still more than you can handle, make sure your next conversation is a prayer. God will lead you to whomever it is you need to speak in order to make it through.

After calling on Jesus, Peter made it to shore safely. After praying and a few tears, I found myself a frequent visitor to my professor's office during office hours. Somehow I passed that class and graduated with my master's degree. I'm a living witness - God uses failure to lift us up!

Tuesday - Your Challenge and a Teaching Tip

Challenge: This week, encourage some student who hasn't been living up to her or his potential in the classroom. Starting with words of kindness, offer assistance as you see fit. Additionally, find someone who teaches better than you in some way and, through conversation and/ or demonstration, glean a new technique or pedagogical skill. Get out of your comfort zone and try something new. It's a double challenge this week, but you can do it!

Teaching Tip: No matter how long you've been teaching, resist the urge to think you know everything. The old adage, "If you're the smartest person in the room, you're in the wrong room" still holds true. Whether through colleagues, classes, online resources, or another type of professional development, make sure you consistently connect with others who can assist you in doing your job better.

Wednesday - Time in the Word

Matthew 14:22-32

Thursday - Prayer

Lord, we thank You for times when You allow us to fail. Far too often it's when we fall down that we finally look up to You. Please forgive us for when we've been stubborn, unfocused, or arrogant enough to think that we've got things under control. Thank You for being the God who sits high and still looks low. Give us the strength we need throughout this week to take risks - not just in getting help from others, but also giving assistance where we can. Indeed, it is more blessed to give than to receive. Take us by the hand and lead us where we need to go one step at a time, with our eyes firmly fixed on You. This is our humble prayer in Jesus' name, amen.

Friday - Reflection

How was your week? Did you complete the challenge? What lessons did you learn? What did you see God do this week?

_____

_____

_____

_____

Do You See What I See?

_____

_____

_____

Week 4

Stop Teaching!

Memory Verse - "Be still, and know that I am God."
Psalm 46:10

"Stop. Close your mouth. Go sit down."

Wait a minute, this is *my* classroom. Who would dare speak to *me* like this while I taught AP Calculus? Even more than that, this was one of *my* favorite subjects to teach.

"Sit down."

I stopped in my tracks as I realized God was changing how I "taught." It was time for me to move from being the sage on the stage to the guide on the side.

The students in this Calculus course had been working diligently and now came a question that would cause them to use nearly everything they'd learned in their entire Mathematics career. I enjoyed letting them struggle a bit, then stepping in right on time to save them. It was right then when I clearly heard God speak, telling me my help was no longer needed. I remember responding in my head that if I didn't start now, we wouldn't finish before the period ended. Besides, I *really* liked this question!

Do You See What I See?

I reluctantly followed God's directive, then watched as each student engaged more than they had the entire year. They asked me questions but soon realized they were going to have to do this without my help. In the end, it took them about 3 times as long as my lesson plans had scheduled, but they were 10 times better for it because *they* had answered the question themselves. After that, they felt empowered to answer nearly all the questions in the course without my help. Delmás Campbell, one of mentors, often says, "Self-discovery is more permanent."

Jesus Himself ignored a woman asking for help. She begged for a crumb from the Master's table and initially He acted as though she wasn't even there. Knowing He would supply her need, she never left His side. Ultimately, she received what she'd asked for, but the real lesson was for the disciples. They needed more "self-discovery" into their arrogance and biases. Jesus, the Master teacher, was teaching them - much like I was the student who learned the most in AP Calculus class that day. Using the most unlikely of sources, Jesus will teach those who are willing to listen.

Be on the lookout - Christ is going to teach you something new today!

Tuesday - Your Challenge and a Teaching Tip

Challenge: Resist the urge to control everything in your classroom, especially students' minds. This week, allow their creative juices to flow and give them questions that don't have set or easy answers. In fact, they may have no answer at all. From there let them know that textbooks don't hold all the information about a subject and that learning is a lifelong process. The more you know, the more you realize you don't know.

Teaching Tip: Teaching students to think independently is a crucial skill in the classroom and, even more so, in life. Stretch your students, and maybe yourself, by allowing students to struggle with ideas and questions. Students should be *thinkers, not mere reflectors of others' thoughts* (*Education*, p. 17). It's a delicate balance to have students struggle but not be overwhelmed, and finding that balance is absolutely worthwhile.

Wednesday - Time in the Word

Matthew 15:21-28

Thursday - Prayer

Dear heavenly Father, thank You for the training we've received on how to teach the students before us. Many times, though, the skills required to be successful are located at Your throne of grace. Help us to be still and know that You are God. Let us speak up when we need to and be quiet when it's prudent. As leaders in the classroom who help to mold the minds of tomorrow, give us the patience, the love, the joy, and the gentleness that's necessary for our students to get a glimpse of You through us. Let us keep learning each day from You, the Master Teacher. We ask it all in Jesus' name, amen.

Friday - Reflection

How was your week? Did you complete the challenge? What lessons did you learn? What did you see God do this week?

_____

_____

Do You See What I See?

_____

_____

_____

_____

_____

Week 5

"Just Don't Hit It in the Water..."

Memory Verse - "Finally, brethren, whatever things are true, whatever things are noble, whatever things are just, whatever things are pure, whatever things are lovely, whatever things are of good report, if there is any virtue and if there is anything praiseworthy— meditate on these things."
Philippians 4:8

Just over ten years ago I started playing golf. It's a difficult game for most people, not just because of the physical aspect but also because of the mental aspect. I remember hearing someone say, "The only thing harder than hitting a ball coming at you at 100 miles per hour is hitting one that isn't moving." It took quite some time to get comfortable with the game, but I absolutely love the challenge.

There's one hole in particular that is quite daunting on the golf course where I regularly played. Even if I'm playing well, I know that hole number 8 is not going to be friendly. It's the one with the water. I would estimate having lost about 30 golf balls in that lake.

You see, every time I got to that hole I would tell myself the same thing, "just don't hit the ball in the water." I would repeat this several times right before I hit the ball...into the water. No matter how well or poorly I was playing, the same thing kept happening. I do have good news though. Now, I rarely hit the ball in the water (and, no, it's not just because I moved to Australia).

What finally happened was a bit of great advice from a friend - "Don't focus on what you're not going to do, focus on what you *will* do." Simply put, I hadn't been looking at where I wanted to go, I was just looking at where I didn't want to go and hence ended up exactly where I was focused. Once that changed, the game got easier (notice I said easier, not easy).

A man had been laying on the ground for 38 years when Jesus stopped by and asked a pretty easy question - "Wilt thou be made whole?" He responded by saying he didn't have anyone to help him get into the water. I can't blame him for being negative, but as a teacher I would've liked for him to have actually answered the question. Like me, he was focused on the water when his eyes really should have been looking in a completely different direction. Thankfully Jesus ignored his answer, got him over the whole water thing, and planted his feet firmly on solid ground.

I thank God for His patience with us. My advice to you today is to keep your eyes focused on Him every step of the way.

Tuesday - Your Challenge and a Teaching Tip

Challenge: This week try to use only positive phrases with your students, colleagues, and family. (Interestingly, I initially wrote, "try not to use negative phrases," which is exactly what you shouldn't do.) This will be pretty difficult, and will involve taking a few extra deep breaths when dealing with certain individuals, but it is possible with God's help.

Teaching Tip: One thing I've learned about behavioral modification is that you shouldn't tell the person what not to do but instead tell them what they should do. If I tell someone who doesn't know better, "Don't touch the stove," the probability is high that they'll miss the first word in that command.

Be positive with what you want your students to do. Spend time giving affirmations to students who are doing the right thing and less time on those doing the wrong. Often, students are seeking attention. Once it's established that positive behaviors get more feedback, students tend to fall in line.

Wednesday - Time in the Word

John 5:1-15

Thursday - Prayer

Oh Lord, how easy it is for us to dwell on negative things. We're bombarded with them from every side, whether it's the news of the day or issues that have been affecting us for a while. Yet somehow, through the hope You provided for us through Calvary, we can still smile. We can still have joy. We can still have the peace that surpasses all understanding. Allow us today to look to You, the Author and Finisher of our faith, as we focus on the positive aspects of our situations. Remind us again that ultimately, eternity with You will be ours. For that and so much more we are thankful, in Jesus' name. Amen.

Friday - Reflection

How was your week? Did you complete the challenge? What lessons did you learn? What did you see God do this week?

Do You See What I See?

_____

_____

_____

_____

_____

_____

_____

I Have My Reservations, Part 1

Memory Verse - "For where your treasure is,
there your heart will be also."
Matthew 6:21

'm not sure if my mouth actually dropped open during the pre-week meeting but it might as well have. I had just moved to Jamaica and what my Head of School just said was truly a foreign concept.

"The work day ends at 3:30. You should go home at 3:30. If you're here working regularly past that time we're going to have to talk about it."

Amazing! I immediately thought of where my wife and I could go out to eat. Maybe we could make regular reservations somewhere nice since we'd have the extra time. It would be great to get off from work that early. Coming from a boarding school where I was at school for a minimum of 14 hours a day during the week and about eight hours on weekends (I was single and loved the work, by the way), I didn't know what I would do with myself.

A few months later it hit me that I'd been doing things backwards. I was giving all of best energies to work and leaving the rest for my family. Maybe it was because of all those hours I'd worked when I was single that I thought I needed to overwork. Maybe it was the work culture in the US that pushed me to stay at my job late and feel guilty if I didn't. It took a while, but I finally realized that I needed to reprioritize and keep something in reserve for the things that are most important in life.

Ananias and Sapphira had their reservations as well. Unfortunately for them, their priorities remained in the wrong order. They held something back for themselves that should've been for God. They had promised to give their all, but later demonstrated by their actions that they wanted to do things differently with what God had provided for them. They had forgotten from Whom their blessings had come and gotten lost in trying to serve both God and mammon. It ended up costing them their lives.

Don't let this be you. We do have to work. But, if anything, make sure you keep back enough of your time, energy, and even money to do exactly what God wants you to do.

Tuesday - Your Challenge and a Teaching Tip

Challenge: Take a few moments to have an honest discussion with God about what truly is in your heart. Is He number one or is there another (or others) that have taken priority? This self-reflection is crucial. Take time to prayerfully consider this and start the process of change today. This may mean less time on your phone, leaving some papers to grade until tomorrow, or even missing out on attending an event. However, it'll truly be worth it in the end.

Teaching Tip: When giving a critique, sandwich your conversations with students and their parents with positivity. Start and end the conversation on a positive note, even if the student has done nothing but given trouble the entire year. Keep a positive reserve of information on how students have done, academically and/or behaviorally. Communicating with parents throughout the school year when students do well, not just when they've done something wrong, goes a long way, especially before parent-teacher meetings.

Wednesday - Time in the Word

Acts 5:1-11

Thursday - Prayer

Heavenly Father, there are infinitely many lessons we can learn from Your word and we thank You for still speaking to us through the lives of those who lived long ago. As educators, we need to be lifelong learners, even, and maybe especially, from the mistakes others have made. Give us the wisdom we need to learn these lessons without needing to go through the experience. Our desire is to live for You and have no one or thing come in between. Help us to give 100% to You, knowing that there's no other way to be truly successful. This is our prayer in the matchless name of Jesus Christ. Amen.

Friday - Reflection

How was your week? Did you complete the challenge? What lessons did you learn? What did you see God do this week?

_____

_____

_____

_____

Do You See What I See?

_____

_____

_____

Week 7

I Have My Reservations, Part 2

Memory Verse - "If any of you lacks wisdom, let him ask of God, who
gives to all liberally and without reproach,
and it will be given to him."
James 1:5

I am a man who thoroughly enjoys watching sports. My wife and I had just bought a new TV specifically for me to be able to watch the NBA Finals. It was the end of game 5 and the game was close. There were about 2 minutes left in the 4th quarter when I heard the sound of keys in the front door. I didn't even bother to glance over to see. Then, out of nowhere (again), God decided to speak.

"Turn off the TV. She's more important."

I hesitated for a moment, then grabbed the remote and hit the power button. I gave my wife my full attention as she came in and told me about her day. The conversation only lasted for a few moments but it was crucial, more so for me than for her. I missed a good portion of the game but I learned a much more valuable lesson - I needed to give my full attention to those who are most important. (By the way, we ended up watching the last few moments of the game together.)

Reserving your best energy for what's most important is something that's critical for your relationships. This includes at work, but also with God, family and friends. Once things are out of order in this regard, the stresses of life can easily become overwhelming.

Jesus' disciples had a similar issue. They had been with Jesus for a while but they had yet to properly prioritize their minds. They were giving their energy to others but their relationship with Jesus was lacking. When He needed them to be praying with Him in the garden of Gethsemane they became the Dream Team, where all 11 of them fell asleep. They hadn't reserved their best for what was most important.

It takes a while to break bad habits but it's possible. Make sure you put God, then family, then others things at the top of your list. Save your best for first.

Tuesday - Your Challenge and a Teaching Tip

Challenge: Besides the **absolute** necessities, try not to use your cellphone, internet, or TV. Use the newfound time with God and family or to accomplish something you've wanted to do for quite some time.

Teaching Tip: There's a difference between what's urgent and what's important. Keep the latter at the top of your list. Just because it's urgent doesn't mean it's important. I've been guilty of confusing the two many times. Some things, if not done immediately, won't get done. That's actually okay. What matters is that what's important gets done.

Wednesday - Time in the World

Mark 14:32-42

Thursday - Prayer

Lord, You are a God of relationships. You love us so much that You left everything and gave the same. For that we say thank You. Allow us this week to make extra time for You and for the things that are important. Give us the mindfulness to truly see what You have in store for us to accomplish by helping those in need, for in doing so we are more blessed. Thank You for the connections we have with others. We pray today that You enlarge our territory in this regard, that we might be able to, together with them, glorify Your name. All of this we ask in the righteous name of Your Son, Jesus the Christ. Amen.

Friday - Reflection

How was your week? Did you complete the challenge? What lessons did you learn? What did you see God do this week?

_____

_____

_____

_____

_____

_____

_____

May I Have Your Attention Please?

Memory Verse - "And you will seek Me and find Me, when you search for Me with all your heart."
Jeremiah 29:13

A few students turned around to see who had quietly said it. As we stood in the hallway with our classmates, and with an administrator about to give a message on the PA system, I urged my 7th grade friend Alex Rosenfeld to repeat what he said a little louder. He obliged.

"May I Have Your Attention Please?!"

To his amazement, the entire class turned toward him, awaiting something important. Alex looked like a deer caught in headlights. I laughed heartily. Unfortunately, our teacher, who had been trying to quiet us down for some time, was not amused. Alex got sent to the principal's office. (Sorry, Alex.)

If you've been teaching for a while, you may be able to make this determination within just a few moments of interacting with a student. It may be the student who's always gossiping or always in a fight. It could be the student who is *too* quiet or the one who is constantly making fun of others. It might be the one who never cracks a smile. It manifests itself in myriad ways, but the underlying issue is usually the same - an unhealthy desire for attention.

This isn't the normal attention students usually want and require. This one is rooted in a lack of attention given by those are supposed to provide it from birth. Initially, I thought it was whether there were two parents in the home, but later I realized it was more intricate than that - it's how attentive the parent(s)/guardian(s) are to the child.

Many times we think that students who have little financially are the ones who suffer most in this way. However, I have found that the same problems exist regardless of a students' socioeconomic status. I have titled it "The New ADD - When Wealth Becomes Poverty." It's based on seeing so many students, many of whom have enough material wealth to get through the financial aspect of life without any problem, who lack a familial connection. Their attention deficit disorder is caused by a lack of attention from those they need it from most. They are looking for love but don't know where to find it.

A rich young man came running to Jesus, looking for that Love. He had all the earthly things anyone could want or need but something still was missing and he knew Jesus had it. Unfortunately, he wasn't willing to give up what he had in order to get that which he needed. He had run to Jesus thinking he was rich. Yet he walked away more impoverished than ever before.

All of us need attention. All of us need love. It starts with connecting with Jesus, for He has enough of both to give everyone. May He have Your attention, please?

Tuesday - Your Challenge and a Teaching Tip

Challenge: I hope that Jesus is still atop your priority list from week 6's introspection. This week I want you to spend 5 more minutes in prayer each day than you regularly do. Converse with your Savior, not just talking at Him and asking for things, but thanking Him and praising Him for all He's done, doing, and will do. Give Him a few more minutes of your undivided attention.

Teaching Tip: Start and stay organized. It's better to start each day and week feeling ready to handle the challenges and disruptions that are bound to come than being out of sorts from the beginning. Develop a routine and stick to it as best as possible. Many times teaching can be chaotic. Having the knowledge that something is under control can be very beneficial.

Wednesday - Time in the Word

Luke 18:18-27

Thursday - Prayer

Lord, of the many descriptors of You, the one most people like is Love. We understand what love is through Your word and through Your works. When You became flesh You were singularly focused on Your goal and, with a life replete with prayer, You accomplished it. We know that Your attention was fixed on Your purpose, which was and is to seek and to save us. Help us even now to fix our attention on You, that the things of this world will grow strangely dim in the light of Your glory and grace. Help us to not look back but to press toward the mark for the prize of Your high calling. We ask all this in the inimitable name of Jesus. Amen.

Friday - Reflection

How was your week? Did you complete the challenge? What lessons did you learn? What did you see God do this week?

_____

_____

_____

_____

_____

_____

_____

Staying Alive

Memory Verse - "Your word is a lamp to my feet
and a light to my path."
Psalm 119:105

As director of the Creative Arts Drama Ministry at Pine Forge Academy, I thoroughly enjoyed traveling with the group on bus trips around the United States. There was one trip in particular though, that makes me shake my head every time I think about it.

We decided to leave from Pennsylvania at midnight to arrive at church in North Carolina by 8am. We ministered through skits and a short play in the morning, then a full length play in the afternoon. Afterwards, the students decided they wanted to get back early on Sunday so they could study (amazing!), so we had our chartered bus pick us up. It was a long day and we started our return trip around 11pm.

I had spoken with the driver a few times that day, making sure he knew the plan and where to meet us. When he arrived to take us on the return trip, he looked a little fatigued. As we spoke he mentioned that, instead of sleeping during the day as he was supposed to, he went to visit some friends who lived in the area. As a veteran of driving while asleep (don't ask), I knew this was trouble, but I figured he was a professional so he knew what he was doing.

For a bus with about 50 high school students and 3 chaperones, it was extremely quiet. Everyone, especially me, was exhausted from the long day of activity. I had found a wonderfully comfortable sleeping position at the back of the bus and was looking forward to some good rest. Unfortunately, I soon realized the driver was also semi-conscious. Three times in a matter of minutes I'd heard the wheels of the bus rubbing against the rumble strips, also known as sleeper lines, of the highway. I said to myself, "If I hear the tires one more time, I'm going to have to go to the front and talk to him." My next God-inspired thought was, "There may not be another chance."

I can't remember everything we talked about for the next seven hours, but I still remember that the bus driver was a family man who loved bowling. It took a lot out of me, but we made it to our destination safely.

Jesus spent many nights talking instead of sleeping. Through these conversations with His Father He received enough strength to give His children the opportunity to stay alive and get them home safely. The big difference here is that, in the end, it didn't just take something out of Him. It took His everything.

Sometimes you will be extraordinarily tired. Yet we must remember that there are lives at stake, literally. Too often, people take for granted the impact that one teacher can have in changing someone's life. Be the teacher who advocates for students who might be on the verge of losing everything, even if they don't know it. It's worth the sacrifice.

Tuesday - Your Challenge and a Teaching Tip

Challenge: Choose a student or colleague who is "falling asleep at the wheel." This is an individual who could be doing more but isn't or someone who needs help because there's too much on their plate. Pray for the Holy Spirit to guide you to them and also that they might be receptive to your mentoring. Find a few minutes or so to meet each day to check in on them and another few to pray for them.

Teaching Tip: Students are apt to respond more positively to criticism that's done privately. If a student is insubordinate, it's better to have him/her step outside and wait for you than for you to make a scene in the classroom in front of his/her peers. You might "win" by getting the child to change their behavior for the day, but the underlying issues will probably remain and the student may shut down and not respond to you. Taking just a few moments with them outside, asking them what's wrong and letting them know you care, can make a tremendous difference.

Wednesday - Time in the Word

John 17:1-26

Thursday - Prayer

Lord, Your word says that it's high time to awaken out of sleep. Truly there are times when we have no strength left and we need You to take the wheel. At the same time we ask for Your forgiveness for when we've fallen asleep at the wheel, when we should've had our eyes fixed on the path ahead. We don't want to get distracted or grow weary in well doing and we need Your help to stay awake and focused. There are specific tasks that You have gifted us to accomplish that will not get done if we don't do them. Indeed, You require much from whom much has been given. However, those whom You call You also equip, and for that we are grateful. Let Your light shine brightly through us each day this week, is our prayer in Jesus' name. Amen.

Friday - Reflection

How was your week? Did you complete the challenge? What lessons did you learn? What did you see God do this week?

_____

_____

_____

_____

_____

_____

_____

Week 10

Gas and a Cough Drop

Memory Verse - "The way of a fool is right in his own eyes, But he who heeds counsel is wise."
Proverbs 12:15

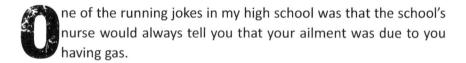ne of the running jokes in my high school was that the school's nurse would always tell you that your ailment was due to you having gas.

Coughing? Oh, that's gas.
Temperature of 105°? It's gas.
Fell down the stairs and you think you broke your foot and three ribs? Classic gas symptoms.

When I began teaching professionally, the school's nurse was also known for one thing. This time it was prescribing cough drops for everything. I distinctly remember asking a student, who clearly wasn't feeling well, if she wanted to go to the nurse. "Mr. Niles...I don't need a cough drop." Ouch. Of course these nurses did much more than they were given credit for doing.

I often spoke with Nurse Leftridge, the school nurse at my first teaching assignment. I recall our discussion not on why she "only prescribed cough drops," but why teachers couldn't simply give them to whichever students they thought needed one. I remember the answer to this day (I also use it to introduce *u*-substitution in my calculus classes, but that's another story). "You can't give out cough drops because coughing could be a symptom of a more serious underlying illness. The student needs to be seen by a trained professional." Mind blown!

Peter and John encountered a man begging for money. This crippled gentleman was looking for a quick release from his pain. He was looking for a cough drop. Somehow, Nurse Peter diagnosed his condition in short order - what He needed was the healing power of the great Physician. With just a simple word of faith, the man was healed.

The devil wants us to only treat symptoms and think we've conquered the deadly disease of sin. Quite frankly, it's easy to look like we're okay when we're anything but. Doing that long enough might even make us believe we're actually okay. We're not. We're wretched, poor, blind, and naked. See the great Physician, Dr. Jesus, today for a full check-up. Then be sure to take whatever He prescribes.

Tuesday - Your Challenge and a Teaching Tip

Challenge: This week make a point to listen to those who haven't reached your professional level. Find at least one person per day and ask them for one random piece of advice or their favorite quote. You're guaranteed to glean some wonderful new insights and ideas.

Teaching Tip: Generally, we teach how we were taught. However, many times it's our students who unwittingly give great pedagogical advice. Listening to how they respond to you and how they teach each other can tell you how to develop your next lesson so that better understanding occurs. Be eager to listen and flexible enough to try things differently.

Wednesday - Time in the Word

Acts 3:1-16

Thursday - Prayer

God, we acknowledge You as the Source of all wisdom. We are certain that Your ways are unsearchable and Your infinite mind is unfathomable. And yet, You still are not only mindful of us but You use us for Your glory. Thank You. Please allow us to be humble enough to help others with what You have given us, and also wise enough to gain wisdom from those with whom we interact. You regularly use human beings, regardless of whether we acknowledge You as Lord or not, to give wisdom to Your children. Teach us again, by any means You see fit, that we might attain a higher level of intimacy with You. In Jesus' name, amen.

Friday - Reflection

How was your week? Did you complete the challenge? What lessons did you learn? What did you see God do this week?

_____

_____

_____

_____

Norman Niles

Say Sorry

Memory Verse - "If My people who are called by My name will humble themselves, and pray and seek My face, and turn from their wicked ways, then I will hear from heaven, and will forgive their sin and heal their land."
2 Chronicles 7:14

ow difficult is it for you to apologize? For me, it used to be nearly impossible.

I'm not sure if you've ever had to carry a half gallon tin can of pineapple juice, but this was a regular occurrence in my house when we had visitors. As a young teenager, I was carrying about four of these cans in a grocery bag, partly to see if I was strong enough to do so. As I wobbled toward the kitchen, I accidentally banged the bag right against my cousin's knee. He screamed in pain and everyone, after checking on him, looked at me for an apology. Somehow the words, "I'm sorry," could not come out of my mouth. To this day I don't know why, but in the moment I had to improvise. I was frozen and all eyes were on me to say one simple word. It never came. I decided that acting like I also got hit in the leg with the cans, then limping the rest of the way was my best option. I laid low the rest of the afternoon.

Years later, I made a huge mistake as a rookie teacher when I publicly told a student to "Shut up!" (Yes, this was the same class that had terrible behavior all year. Still, there's no excuse.) Fortunately I had matured by that time and I privately, then publicly, apologized to her. The class's reaction to my public apology to the young lady was very interesting. Many looked surprised that a teacher would admit fault. In admitting my guilt, I was no longer the "infallible creature" they thought all teachers to be. I became a relatable, faulty, human being to them. Things actually went better with the behavior of the class for the remainder of the year. Humility can be a powerful thing.

Daniel's recorded prayer is one that includes himself as a part of the nation of sinners, although by all accounts he had no role in their sins. His contrite reflection teaches us that, as we intercede for others, we must also look deeply into our own lives. As we do, we'll realize our need to ask God to forgive us for things we shouldn't have done and also for the things we didn't do that we should've. Thank God that He hears and is ever willing to forgive us.

Tuesday - Your Challenge and a Teaching Tip

Challenge: Apologize to someone (or *someones*) this week. You haven't been perfect in your interactions and although it might be 99% the other person's fault, God had called us to the ministry of reconciliation. It'll be difficult (it's called a challenge for a reason), but God provides the strength to do what He wants us to do. We just have to be willing.

Teaching Tip: Students tend to behave better and give more of an effort when they are interacting with those whom they feel they have a connection/relationship. When possible, and without ever crossing your professional boundaries, allow your students to get to know you outside of the classroom or office. Whether it's as a coach, cheering them on at a sporting event, or leading an extracurricular activity or club, try to have students see you as more than a subject teacher or administrator.

Do You See What I See?

Wednesday - Time in the Word

Daniel 9:1-19

Thursday - Prayer

Confession is good for the soul and we thank You Lord for the healing that comes with it. We don't like having to apologize, but we know that these conversations must happen if we are to be like You. Forgive us for the grudges we've held when we ourselves want to be forgiven much more speedily. Forgive us for not following Your directive to have such a forgiving spirit. Strengthen us to be ready to do so even before we're offended. Thank You for Your example and strength. Give us the power this week to forgive and seek forgiveness. We pray this in Jesus' name. Amen.

Friday - Reflection

How was your week? Did you complete the challenge? What lessons did you learn? What did you see God do this week?

_____

_____

_____

_____

Norman Niles

_____

_____

_____

Week 12

I Can't Complain

Memory Verse - "Jesus Christ is the same yesterday,
today, and forever."
Hebrews 13:8

The following is the standard greeting between a very close friend of mine, L. David Harris, and me.

"How's it going, bro?"
"I can't complain."
"Wouldn't help anyway."

I hate complaining. (Wait...am I now complaining about it?) Complaining is contagious and it's most often a symptom of amnesia.

It's human nature to complain when you're tired or hungry. During my first year as the assistant director of my school's drama group, we participated in a youth convention in Atlanta, GA. The trip occurred during our spring break and everyone was tired from the long journey and the shows we had put on throughout the week. The day before our only night off the director told us that we had been asked to put on the show the next evening. He accepted the request and the students were visibly and vocally upset. There would be no nights off.

Throughout the next day I heard the students complaining incessantly. But God works in mysterious ways. At the end of the show that evening, our best production by far, the audience was visibly touched and we ourselves were blessed immensely. As we talked together afterward, I was moved by the Holy Spirit to chide the students for complaining. How could we have so easily forgotten what God had done for us? How could we have been so selfish as to complain about ministering?

The newly freed Israelites had done the same thing. They had just walked through the Red Sea and then complained about not having water. Can you believe that? How ungrateful and forgetful can people be? God, in His mercy, didn't send them back the way they came!

Amazingly, we often do the same thing. We easily forget the miracles God just performed for us and complain about our current situation. Yet complaining is a smack in God's face. Before we do so again, let's take the time to remember all He's done for us in the past and all He has planned for us in the future. Jesus is the same everyday - He'll never leave us nor forsake us. There's no reason to complain.

Tuesday - Your Challenge and a Teaching Tip

Challenge: This week's challenge is simple and extremely difficult - don't complain about anything. This includes bad drivers on the road, your spouse or children being late, your administrator making a "terrible" decision, or any other occurrence that arises. Recalling what God has done and knowing that He's still in control, use that energy and time to find solutions instead. No complaints!

Teaching Tip: Allow students to struggle a bit with a difficult task that you're certain they can handle. Once they've completed it, be sure to remind them of the process that it takes to succeed. Encourage them to be positive during the process. This produces confidence and resilience.

Do You See What I See?

Wednesday - Time in the Word

Exodus 15:22 - 16:3

Thursday - Prayer

Lord, help our minds to recall more quickly and easily the things You've done for us in the past. Keep us from complaining about the things we can't control and turn our minds to You and the path on which You're leading us. Keep our eyes fixed on that path. Let us not, like the Israelites of old, waste years doing what could've been done in months, except our unfaithful, complaining, forgetful hearts get in Your way. Even when others around us are doing so, help us to resist and proclaim You as the solution to all our problems. This we ask in the never-failing name of Jesus Christ. Amen.

Friday - Reflection

How was your week? Did you complete the challenge? What lessons did you learn? What did you see God do this week?

_____

_____

_____

_____

Norman Niles

_____

_____

_____

True or False?

Memory Verse - "Therefore take up the whole armor of God, that you may be able to withstand in the evil day, and having done all, to stand."
Ephesians 6:13

He was the best quiz master I've ever heard. Each night of the youth evangelistic series, he would ask five true or false questions about the previous night's sermon. Mind you, these weren't easy questions - you had to listen intently in order to decipher the intricacies of what was being posited. However, the most difficult aspect was resisting the "hint" he provided after some of the questions were asked. These short statements of so-called assistance would sound like one of the following:

"And the answer to that question is true..."
"Of course we're certain that the answer is true.."
"We all know the answer to *this* question is true..."

After a pregnant pause of exactly the right length of time to contemplate, I would then acquiesce to the fact that he was indeed giving away the answer and subsequently mark *True* on the card. Immediately thereafter he would say:

"...or False!"

He knew we had golf pencils (the ones without erasers) so there was no going back. I was there every night for two weeks. Somehow I never got all five questions right.

Critical thinking and resisting peer pressure are crucial skills not just for students, but for adults as well. How many times have you known to do the right thing but because someone else was around you ended up not doing it? How many times have we made mistakes or even believed and shared false information because we didn't take the time to really research and think about it?

The Hebrews had the same issue during Elijah's time when everyone seemed to be following false gods. Even in the midst of a three and a half year drought, no one seemed to turn back to God. When Elijah issued the challenge on Mt. Carmel, asking God's people whom they believed to be God, the people didn't even answer. They left a true or false question blank!

As you read the story this week, take time to analyze what you would have done in this situation (or even what you've done in similar situations where God's name is at stake). Pray that God gives you the will and the strength to stand for truth, though the heavens may fall.

Tuesday - Your Challenge and a Teaching Tip

Challenge: This week is the Show and Tell Challenge! Whether online or in person, tell someone who doesn't know that you're a Christian about Jesus. More importantly, show that you are a Christian by your love. Through a kind word or deed, use your influence to demonstrate God's love. It's been said that a life lived demonstrating the power of Christ is more powerful than any sermon that can be preached.

Do You See What I See?

Teaching Tip: This tip has saved me a good amount of time over the years. For exams that are several pages in length, it may save you time if you write at the bottom of each page how many points were lost on that page. At the end, tally those points and subtract from the total. I got this one from my advisor during my student teaching. Thanks, Mrs. Mitchell!

Wednesday - Time in the Word

1 Kings 18:20-39

Thursday - Prayer

Lord, we thank You for being the Way, the Truth, and the Life. We thank You for access to the throne of grace where we can receive mercy and grace in our time of need. Today we ask for the boldness we need to not be silent when we hear Your Holy Spirit telling us to speak. Allow us to be moved to speak a word of love and hope to someone who needs to hear of You. Help us to seek and take these opportunities to tell of Your goodness and the peace You alone can give. Give us the strength to resist the pressure and excuses that so easily arise, and replace it with power from on high. Lead, guide, and direct us for Your cause and for Your glory, we pray in Jesus' name. Amen.

Friday - Reflection

How was your week? Did you complete the challenge? What lessons did you learn? What did you see God do this week?

_____

_____

_____

_____

_____

_____

Jesus is the Answer

Memory Verse - "'It shall come to pass that before they call, I will answer; and while they are still speaking, I will hear.'"
Isaiah 65:24

One of the rules of life in the classroom is that things will get lost. Pencils, homework, notebooks, you name it. One year I ended up doing an experiment with students who had lost things. When they would ask if I had seen their lost item I would instantly respond with, "Have you prayed about it?" After they all said they hadn't, I replied, "Well, then you're not really trying to find it." It was awesome to see students pausing to pray for things like finding a writing utensil. If they prayed about such little things they would hopefully do the same with the bigger things. Jesus is the answer.

As the number of students asking me about misplaced articles increased, I began to see how quickly God would respond. The first student can back the next day and said he found it. The next came back within a couple of hours, and the following day, the student reacquired her item in under an hour. The next young lady took less than a minute! Note that I only started the timer after they had prayed. After one student found his item in under 30 seconds I figured the experiment was over. God smiled and said, "Watch this."

As we were about to start class with a prayer, one student requested that we pray that she finds her lost notebook. "You mean the pink one you always carry around?" inquired a classmate. "It's in my room. You left it there last night." A slow grin came across my face as God reminded me of our verse for the week - even before we call, He's already answered.

What would you do if one of your students wrote "Jesus" as the answer to every question on your exam? Would they at least get partial credit? (In fact, I had a student do that for a few questions on a Math test. I asked them to be more specific.)

In life outside the classroom, though, we can always use this Answer. The question then becomes, why would we ever not use this "cheat code?" If we have the Answer to all of life's questions and questionings, how foolish would we have to be to not use it? I'm reminded of our Scripture passage for this week where God tells us that He's placed life and death in front of us and we have a choice between the two. Then He actually bothers to tell us the answer to this near idiot-proof question - Choose life! It is my hope that we more fully acknowledge and utilize the power we have to get through all the trials of daily life by talking with the Master Teacher - the One who has and who is the Answer.

Tuesday - Your Challenge and a Teaching Tip

Challenge: This week, write down a few prayer requests - some big and some small - and see how long God takes to answer. It's important to know that sometimes God does respond in a way we don't like but He does still respond. Also, continue praying about it until you do get a response. I hope this challenge will renew your faith in our God who still hears and answers the cries of His children.

Teaching Tip: Students often will hide behind others' answers. When teaching, try to ensure every student knows the answer before moving on. For activities or questions that have multiple steps, provide enough questions so that students stay busy while you check that each student can answer at least one part correctly. Start by checking the students you know will have the most difficulty and don't leave their desk until they've completed and understood one question. Soon students will know they cannot hide and also that you care enough to take the time to make sure they are learning.

Wednesday - Time in the Word

Deuteronomy 30:15-20

Thursday - Prayer

Before any problem existed, You, oh Lord, were the solution. Your word says that Jesus is the Lamb slain before the foundation of the world. You, through the sacrifice of Your Son, fixed a problem of our making that no one else could. Thank You, Lord. Forgive us for having too much pride in our own strength. Help us to seek You for all of the issues we face. Give us the humility to accept Your answers and the strength to go through this character-building process. You long to hear from us and You want to answer us. Remove the hindrances so that before there are any issues, we're trusting in You. Even as issues arise, continue to keep us close to You. After the issues are resolved, remind us to praise You and know that You never change. For being such a loving, answering, and life-giving Savior, we say thank You in Jesus' name. Amen.

Friday - Reflection

How was your week? Did you complete the challenge? What lessons did you learn? What did you see God do this week?

_____

_____

_____

_____

_____

_____

_____

Week 15

Visiting Ours

Memory Verse - "And the second is like it: 'You shall love your neighbor as yourself.'"
Matthew 22:39

F un" would probably not be the word used by anyone to describe surgery. Somehow I figured mine wouldn't be so bad, especially since it was minor, outpatient surgery. Once you made it through the procedure it should be smooth sailing from then on, right? Boy, was I wrong.

As a certified workaholic, my knee surgery to repair a torn meniscus was not something to which I was looking forward. But again, it was quick so I figured I'd be back on my feet soon thereafter. I'm not sure if there are degrees of wrongness (not a real word), but I think I got close to the highest level. My leg was immobilized for two weeks. It was torture trying to get around but more than that, I didn't like *needing* help.

It was the lack of autonomy that got to me the most. Even as comforting as it was to have people to help, I liked relying on myself for most things. For example, I didn't like asking anyone to go to the kitchen and pour a bowl of cereal for me (especially since the proportions would inevitably be incorrect. And for the record, the cereal *must* go in before the milk.). I wanted to do it myself, but I couldn't. For someone who prides himself on being independent, this almost seemed like a curse.

That need for assistance however, paled in comparison to the loneliness that comes from almost being bedridden. I distinctly remember being on the verge of depression one afternoon, with my leg up on the sofa and absolutely nothing to do and no one to talk to for the third day in a row. Suddenly, there was a knock on the door. I hobbled/hopped over to the door and two friends were there to say hello. They only stopped by for about 20 minutes but that may have saved my life. It's something I won't ever forget.

Visiting our friends and relatives is crucially important, especially in their time of need. Christ goes even further however, telling us to visit our neighbors, which includes people we don't know but we're sure have a need. Oh, what it means to be a disciple of Christ. We may not be doctors, but we've been given the power to save lives.

Tuesday - Your Challenge and a Teaching Tip

Challenge: Find time this week to visit a nursing home, prison, halfway house, women's shelter, or homeless shelter. Spend time talking with people, making sure they feel heard and valued. If possible, add this to your weekly or monthly schedule. It'll be a blessing to everyone involved.

Teaching Tip: Having students go outside the classroom is vitally important to their seeing the relevance of your class. Make time for field trips, even if it means visiting the classroom next door or just going outside in nature. Breaking up the monotony of being inside the same four walls each day is something teachers and students enjoy.

Do You See What I See?

Wednesday - Time in the Word

Matthew 25:31-46

Thursday - Prayer

Lord, You left heaven to visit us. You gave up the glory of heaven to give us hope. Truly, what is man that You are mindful of him, and the son of man that You visit him? We are unworthy and so we express our gratitude not just in words, but in deeds. You commanded us to love our neighbor as ourselves and although we have missed too many opportunities before, help us today to not miss a single one. Show us Your plan for each day this week from start to finish. Tell us whom we need to visit, not looking at the hours, but recognizing them as ours - our brothers and sisters in You. Allow us to be receptive to Your Holy Spirit's leading so that someone in eternity will be able to point to this time as when they received their salvation. This is our prayer in Jesus' name, amen.

Friday - Reflection

How was your week? Did you complete the challenge? What lessons did you learn? What did you see God do this week?

_____

_____

_____

Norman Niles

---

13 Years is a Long Time

Memory Verse - "Then Jesus said, 'Father, forgive them, for they do not know what they do.'"
Luke 23:34

The sound of two old women weeping in each other's arms forced me to look in their direction. I had just finished the last appeal after preaching for a two-week youth evangelistic series. These ladies were far from the target audience but somehow God used me to end something that had gone on for far too long.

Thirteen years was about the median age of the intended audience. Thirteen years is one year longer than three presidential terms in the United States of America. Thirteen years is the number of years I taught Mathematics before writing this devotional. Thirteen years is the time it usually takes between beginning kindergarten and graduating from high school. Thirteen years is a long time and it's how long these two old Jamaican ladies had been going to the same church while holding a grudge and not speaking a single word to one another. 13 Years.

I was nearly moved to tears as I was forced into a three-way hug when I went to investigate the ruckus. As we prayed together, I thanked God for allowing these two to finally come together and make amends. I'm not sure if they even recall what initiated the hostility, but that day was a day of celebration. The weight of this burden wrought by

Satan had been lifted. Make no mistake - they were both destined for eternal damnation if they had gone to their graves without forgiving one another. Now these two were again candidates for the kingdom.

I realized that when Jesus uttered the words, "Father, forgive them for they know not what they do," He was asking for forgiveness for people who had not yet repented. Imagine that. What would it be like to forgive others *before* they trespassed against us? What kind of heart would you have to have to be ready to reconcile with someone before a hurt occurred and before anyone apologized? The answer - we'd have to have a heart like His.

I pray that God removes our hard-heartedness and replaces it with one just like His.

Tuesday - Your Challenge and a Teaching Tip

Challenge: One of the most difficult things in life is to forgive someone. Yes, it's cathartic in that we are able to not be controlled emotionally by the incident and/or the individual(s), but no one said it was easy. This week the challenge is simple - Forgive Everyone. Whether it's a student, parent, your mother, father, long-time friend, acquaintance, person who gossiped about you in high school, or a distant relative, forgive them. It can be an extremely difficult process, but now is the time to begin. If you're particularly struggling with this you may want to prayerfully read this week's scriptural passage more than once.

Teaching Tip: First impressions of students are often incorrect. Students who may appear aloof on the first day may end up being the best in your class. Be mindful to give each student myriad opportunities to demonstrate his/her best work and behavior. Expect them to do well each day and see the results.

Wednesday - Time in the Word

Matthew 18:21-35

Thursday - Prayer

Lord, it seems to be easier to ask for forgiveness than to extend it to others, but we know we need to do both. You've told us that the same way we forgive others is the same way You will forgive us. It takes supernatural power to do this and so we come to You for an extra portion of grace and mercy. Give us a heart that forgives, one that's ready to forgive others no matter the infraction. And as we extend this to others, release our burdens and give us the peace that surpasses all human understanding. We pray this in Jesus' name. Amen.

Friday - Reflection

How was your week? Did you complete the challenge? What lessons did you learn? What did you see God do this week?

_____

_____

_____

_____

_____

Can These Bones Live?

Memory Verse - "For the Lord Himself will descend from heaven with a shout, with the voice of an archangel, and with the trumpet of God. And the dead in Christ will rise first."
1 Thessalonians 4:16

Some caskets are heavier than others.

I don't have any biological daughters but I do have many whom I call mine from my days teaching at a boarding school. There are seven in particular who are quite close.

Initially, when two of them approached me to be their "campus dad," I was hesitant. Then I came to a conclusion. As we were about to join others for a dinner off-campus, I had mulled it over enough. The subsequent conversation went something like this.

"Ladies, I've thought it over and I've decided that I'm not going to be able to be your campus father."

"Ok, dad."
"Ok, father."

Maybe I wasn't clear..
"No, no. I'm NOT going to be your campus father."

"Ok. Can we go inside now, dad?"
"Yes, father. We're very hungry."

And with that, I realized that I hadn't really been given a choice. I closed my aghast mouth and a small grin replaced it. I thought to myself, "Well, I guess I have two kids now."

Sadly, this exchange, along the first line of this devotion, were messages that were shared at one of their funerals. She was only 29 and died of complications with leukemia. She was engaged to be married and her wedding date had been set for just four months after her passing. Her fiance is a great young man whom I had taught and coached. It was, and still is, one of the saddest moments of my life. Children aren't supposed to die before their parents.

I share this story with you because you probably have experienced the sting of death in some way. Yet somehow there is hope after heartache. Somehow in the midst of death and devastation God demonstrates His power and reminds us of His plan.

Joseph had been dead for over 400 years when the Israelites were freed from Egypt. Each day of their slavery, his bones were a physical reminder that God had promised that their current situation was only temporary. Could these old bones live? Yes, was the resounding answer, for they pointed to life in the promised land.

I look forward to that promised land where there will be no more death or sorrow or mourning, for the former things will have passed away. Let the passing away of those close to us be a reminder that Jesus is truly coming soon. Let it also motivate us to live our lives as if each day is our last.

Do You See What I See?

Tuesday - Your Challenge and a Teaching Tip

Challenge: Carpe diem is an oft overused phrase that means *Seize the day*, but it's quite appropriate at this time. This week don't focus on the mistakes of the past nor the stresses of the future, but seize today as best you can. Make a list of things you want to accomplish within the next year and come up with pragmatic, attainable ways to reach those goals on a daily basis. Want to lose weight? Stop eating late and exercise more. Want to write a book? Find someone who will hold you to your timeline. There's no time like the present. Seize today!

Teaching Tip: Research has shown that what is said at the start and end of a presentation is what is recalled in the long-term memory more easily, while the information in between is relegated to the short term (Westmaas, 2017). With that, you want to start and end each class with the objectives. Knowing where they're going helps students during the process and they feel very accomplished once they reach their destination successfully.

Wednesday - Time in the Word

Ezekiel 37:1-14

Thursday - Prayer

Lord, death is something You never intended. Yet, as a result of our sin, it's an inevitable part of our lives this side of heaven. It's been said that time heals all wounds, but sometimes it feels like the wound of death will never truly heal. Our hearts are heavy every time we remember our loved ones who are no longer with us. Yet in those moments we are reassured by Your Word that this isn't the end and that there is hope. These bones, that trusted You to the grave, will indeed rise to live again. Help us daily to be faithful. Let us trust You more fully in these times so that our lives can be living testimonies for You. And one day soon, let all of us repeat together the glorious refrain from Your word, "Behold, this is our God! We have waited and He has come to save us. This is our Lord. We have waited for Him. Let us be glad and rejoice in His salvation!" We pray all this in the quickening name of Jesus Christ. Amen.

Friday - Reflection

How was your week? Did you complete the challenge? What lessons did you learn? What did you see God do this week?

_____

_____

_____

_____

_____

_____

_____

Looking for Love in All the Wrong Places

Memory Verse - "Beloved, let us love one another, for love is of God; and everyone who loves is born of God and knows God."
1 John 4:7

It was the single most difficult question I've been asked in a class-room. I was teaching religion and the subject was marriage, family and love, when one young lady raised her hand and audibly que-ried, "How can I get into a loving relationship if I've never seen one?" Regrettably, the answer was neither in my head nor in the textbook that day.

Incredibly, another student around that same time told me she didn't have a relationship with her father and had only received one card from him. It was a birthday card she received when she turned 14. Inside he wrote how happy he was that he wasn't around because he had heard that she was a terrible child. I had to hold back my tears even as they flowed down her cheeks.

Missing a parent's love or living in a home where love is absent can exponentially increase the likelihood that a child looks for love in the wrong places. This can manifest itself in choosing to be in bad relation-ships or making bad choices in them, staying away from relationships altogether and intentionally drowning oneself in work, or even trying things like drugs and alcohol to fill the void. None of these things can replace what we are all seeking - true Love.

Mary Magdalene literally went looking for Love in the wrong place. She had gone to Jesus' tomb but He was no longer there. I like how the King James version writes how the two angels' questioned her - "Why seek ye the living among the dead?" Death couldn't hold Love back! No matter how bleak the situation looked, Love was going to find a way.

It took me a few years but the Lord finally gave me an answer to the first young lady's question. You can't look to man for the perfect example of love. That's only found in Jesus. Love is a choice and it demands sacrifice. Jesus chose to love us all the way to Calvary's cross. Now He wants us to share that sacrificial Love with a world that's dying for it. By the way, I'm thankful for these two ladies. I've kept up with them and, like Mary of old, they have indeed been able to find Love, in the truest sense of the word. I hope you are able to do the same.

Tuesday - Your Challenge and a Teaching Tip

Challenge: For years I've shared with students a phrase that, for me, encapsulates the meaning of life: "Find Love, then love like Love loves." This week your challenge is to love your students, colleagues, administrators, friends, and enemies like Jesus does. This means adding them to your prayer list. This means taking extra time to send a message or call them. This means donating to a cause to assist them. This means loving them like Jesus does.

Teaching Tip: Students "don't care how much you know until they know how much you care" is a motivational phrase for teachers and other educators who want to be known and remembered for more than just the subject(s) they teach or job they perform. Be intentional and, if possible, vocal with your students that you didn't go into education for the money (has anyone?), but because you care about them and their success. This simple act can make all the difference in the world to your students.

Wednesday - Time in the Word

Luke 23:55 - 24:12

Thursday - Prayer

Lord, it's a wonderful thing to know You and the love You continually provide. There is no love without You because You are love. There is no fear in love for Your love is perfect as it casts out all fear. Help us to see You more clearly and love you and our neighbors more dearly. The two greatest commandments are to love You and to love people. As You have said, there's no greater love than to lay down one's life for a friend. Giving up our desires is difficult at times, but we thank You for making it possible. One moment at a time, allow us to draw closer to You, that we might love like Love loves. This we pray, in the loving name of Jesus, amen.

Friday - Reflection

How was your week? Did you complete the challenge? What lessons did you learn? What did you see God do this week?

_____

_____

_____

_____

_____

_____

_____

For Who? For What?

Memory Verse - "And let us not grow weary while doing good, for in due season we shall reap if we do not lose heart."
Galatians 6:9

Growing up in Philadelphia there's a requirement to be a football fan. More specifically, you must root for the Eagles and hate, sorry, loathe the Dallas Cowboys. We're a city that's used to losing, complaining about it, then looking forward to the next year when we'll finally win it all. (It *actually* happened in 2018.)

Although we lose quite a lot more than we win, there's one thing that is an absolute must for professional athletes in Philly - full effort. The most beloved players may never have won a championship, but because of the way they played their respective sports they are forever heroes in our hearts.

I remember in the 90s, one play in particular when Ricky Watters, a member of the Eagles, decided not to give his all. He decided it was better to pull in his arms, slow down, and not catch the ball instead of stretching out to catch it and probably getting viciously hit by the other team.

Nearly all of Philly was in an uproar the next day. It wasn't simply because he didn't do everything he could on that play (at that point in the game we had zero chance of winning). In fact, it was probably the right decision on his part. However, it was what he said in the press conference after the game when asked why he didn't put it all on the line that outraged the team's fanbase.

"For who? For what?" he replied with indignation.

Radio waves and water cooler conversations called his name in disgust for years afterwards. After all, he was making millions of dollars. Philadelphians, who live in a blue-collar city, expect to get their hard-earned money's worth when they attend sporting events.

I imagine Satan attempting to put the doubt enveloped in those questions in Jesus' ear as He went to the cross - "It's nearly over. These people won't even bother to accept Your sacrifice. Look around at them. They are screaming for You to die. These are the same ones who yelled 'Hosanna in the highest!' just a couple of days ago. They're never going to change. Are You really going to go through with this...For who?! For what?!"

Jesus lifts His eyes and, looking past the accuser of the brethren, looks down through time to see you. As He fully extends His arms on the cross, and as nails are driven into His hands and feet, He responds with your name on His lips. "For you. Because I love you more than anything."

Tuesday - Your Challenge and a Teaching Tip

Challenge: Take a moment this week to write down your "why." Remember why you are doing what you do. When times get tough, and they will, find the place where you've tucked this note away, whisper a prayer, and get on with the work to which God has called you.

Do You See What I See?

Teaching Tip: Eat properly and exercise often, for your health is your wealth. If practical, allow your students to know your health goals and have them follow you on your journey (they are great accountability partners). This will foster good conversations and subtly instill in them how important it is to take care of yourself so that you can be at your best.

Wednesday - Time in the Word

Luke 23:1-25

Thursday - Prayer

Lord, the cross will always represent the love You have for us. But neither Your outstretched arms nor Your unfailing love remained there. You arose from the dead that we might have life eternal and for that our thanks will be everlasting. And because You love us more than life, help us to live life optimally - helping others even as we improve our health each day. Give us minds to remember that we haven't only been given gifts from You, but we have also been charged to use them for Your glory. And when there seems to be no reason to go on, help us to remember You as our Reason and the Source of our strength. In Jesus' name, amen.

Friday - Reflection

How was your week? Did you complete the challenge? What lessons did you learn? What did you see God do this week?

Norman Niles

_____

_____

_____

_____

_____

_____

A Break is a Break

Memory Verse - "And He said to them, 'The Sabbath was made for man, and not man for the Sabbath.'"
Mark 2:27

Everyone loves a true vacation. I'm not talking about the ones where you have to cook and clean up afterwards. I'm talking about the ones where you forget what day and time it is and you don't care to ask. I'm talking about the ones where you come back and people don't recognize you because you look and feel like a different person. I'm talking about a *real* vacation.

You deserve a vacation. I'm not sure if you can afford one of the aforementioned types of vacations but you, as an educator, definitely need one. We look forward to the breaks during the school year even more than students do. Wayne Henry, one of my good friends and colleagues who sometimes talks in riddles, taught me a lesson one year just before a break. He walked into my room and said, "Niles! A break is a break." The quizzical look on my face let him know this wasn't a profound statement. He then said it again and left the room. It took me a while but I then had my "Aha!" moment - A break *is* a break! I finally realized that, as I needed a vacation, the students needed one too. From that point, unless absolutely necessary, I stopped giving work to students over breaks.

We all need a break. Jesus, our Designer, made us this way. This is part of the reason why He created the Sabbath. God didn't need to rest on the seventh day, He was giving us an example to follow. Imagine getting away from all your work for 24 hours every week and spending time with the One who loves you the most. This is what God tells us to do.

Even more than resting, take the time to help others during this day. Jesus, to the chagrin of many so-called religious people, lifted many burdens on the Sabbath. He healed the crippled, gave sight to the blind, and drove out evil spirits on the seventh day. These were burdens that were long-standing. Burdens that were too heavy to bear any longer. Burdens that needed immediate removal. If you let Him, God will use you to help others be free from their burdens...and He'll remove yours too.

Tuesday - Your Challenge and a Teaching Tip

Challenge: Contrary to what many people do, it's better to put gas in a vehicle before it hits empty rather than to see how far you can go on a tank. Your challenge is to take a Sabbath. Refill your tank weekly by taking 24 hours away from the stresses of life and focus on God and family. It might be difficult at first, but you'll soon reap great dividends.

Teaching Tip: Teachers are often expected to do more than what seems humanly possible. Hence, managing expectations is a crucial skill for your sanity. Saying "No" to some things is okay and actually necessary in many instances. You might feel bad doing so, but you will need to in order to be balanced. Neil Thomas says it best - "Excellence is not intemperance."

Do You See What I See?

Wednesday - Time in the Word

Luke 6:1-11

Thursday - Prayer

O God, we thank You for being so mindful of us that You tell us to take breaks. You want us to commune with You. Thank You for also never taking a break from us, despite our sinful and intemperate ways. Give us the plan we need to be balanced and then the strength and will-power to actualize it. Too often we know what to do but we end up not doing it. Break that cycle, Lord, and again, help us to make time for the things which are most important - starting with our relationship with You. This we ask in Jesus' name, amen.

Friday - Reflection

How was your week? Did you complete the challenge? What lessons did you learn? What did you see God do this week?

_____

_____

_____

_____

_____

Special Holiday Devotion

R.U.N.

Memory Verse - "Therefore we also, since we are surrounded by so great a cloud of witnesses, let us lay aside every weight, and the sin which so easily ensnares us, and let us run with endurance the race that is set before us, looking unto Jesus, the author and finisher of our faith, who for the joy that was set before Him endured the cross, despising the shame, and has sat down at the right hand of the throne of God."
Hebrews 12:1-2

For years this stood as the longest day of my life (taking care of a baby full-time changes things). I was a senior in high school and I had just completed an AP Spanish exam for which I had studied into the morning hours. Afterwards we had a track meet and I was slated to run the maximum number of events allowed by a single student. These weren't short races either. What made matters worse was that it was an extremely hot day - so much so that teams hid under the metal bleachers to get out of the sun.

We had made it to the last race, the 4x400, where four members of each team run one lap of the track. I was extremely tired and not particularly interested in running anymore. I was designated to run the anchor leg, the last of the four runners for my team. Mr. Woods, our coach, brought us together and said the scores were so close that whichever team won this race would win the track meet. My secret hope was that my teammates would either get a large lead so I could run an easy race or be so far behind that I could relax.

My three teammates ran using different styles. The first had a big lead and lost it. The second lagged behind but caught up, while the third kept pace with the two other teams in the lead. As he was halfway through, I said to myself, "These guys are gonna *make* me run today!" It was an extremely close race. By the time I received the baton and taken one step I had gone from third place to first place. It was neck and neck..and neck.

As I ran through the first half of the race I could hear the footsteps of the other two runners interchanging behind me. One thing you can never do in a race is look back, but I knew they were almost literally on my heels.

Our coach had us practice something different during the week before this race. He said we were to run "negatives," where we would run the second half of the race *faster* than the first half. When I got 200 meters in, I pushed myself just like we had practiced. Unfortunately, the bleachers full of students were on that side of the track so I could no longer hear the footsteps behind me. I had no way of knowing how close the others were to catching me.

I ran as fast as I could. Then, with about 50 meters to go, the unthinkable happened. My body stopped responding to my mind. My form broke and my legs and arms started to swing incorrectly. I was stumbling toward the finish line, but I knew I had to finish. I finally leaned across the line and used my peripheral vision to see which place I was in...First! As my teammates ran onto the track to congratulate me, I looked back only to see the two competitors who had been right behind me to now still have about 40 meters left. I looked at the teammates and said, "Why did y'all make me run so fast?!"

Do You See What I See?

My acronym for RUN is
Respice Finem - Keep the End in View
be **U**nconventional
Never quit

Respice Finem. As the school year gets ready to begin again be sure to keep the end in view. Stay motivated by your purpose and your gifts. Recall why you started teaching and be reenergized by it.

Be Unconventional. Run a negative - do the second half of the year better than the first. Yes, just thinking about it can make you feel tired, but God will give you the strength. He's done it for me more times than I can count.

Never quit. Even when you feel there's nothing left in you to give, keep pushing towards the end. As stated in a call and response from *Remember the Titans* (2000),
"What is pain?" "French bread!"
"What is fatigue?" "Army gear!"
"Will you ever quit?!" "No! We want some mo'! We want some mo'! We want some mo'!!"

Keep RUNning - God will take you through it all - one day and one step at a time.

Week 21

Swimming Lessons

Memory Verse - "But without faith it is impossible to please Him, he who comes to God must believe that He is, and that He is a rewarder of those who diligently seek Him."
Hebrews 11:6

You know how to swim? Jump."

We had taken a group of campers to a water park and there was about 5 minutes left before we had to leave. Counselor Kerimah and I were rounding up our troops when we saw it - an approximately three-story high cliff that you could jump off into deep water. We looked at each other and said, "Let's do it!"

We hurriedly got into the line that paradoxically moved quickly and slowly at the same time. As we approached this "ride," we saw the water park employee giving instructions at the top of the cliff. To the pairs of people who were next to jump on either side of him he was simply repeating the quote that begins this devotion. What was most interesting to me was how he was calmly leaning on the desk behind him. I noticed there were words on the front of the desk that he was blocking. As I got closer, I realized these were the written safety instructions for jumping! I started getting a little nervous..

The line was getting shorter as he repeated the same question to every pair. They either nodded or said yes before they took off. However, when the counselor and I got to the front of the line, he did something different. He furrowed his brow, glanced at us, then skipped the question altogether. "Jump!" is all he said to us.

I can swim, but this was something I'd never done. As I started to ponder how this made any sense whatsoever, I said to myself, "If I don't do this now, I won't ev..." In the middle of this thought I had somehow already taken three running steps and now I was in midair. What an exhilarating feeling! And, an added bonus, I lived to tell the story.

Taking a leap of faith requires us to leave the calculations behind. Sometimes it requires leaving people behind as well. Ruth knew this. After losing her husband and with no prospects from her mother-in-law's family in sight, she had the opportunity to leave a foreign land and return home to safety. Yet, she chose to skip Naomi's instructions and take her own leap of faith. The difference here is that she wasn't sure if she'd sink or swim - she just jumped.

God wants you to take this type of leap. The leap where you take a running start not knowing what will happen next. The leap that has you flying towards a brand new experience. The leap where you're completely dependent on Christ. Don't worry, He won't let you drown.

Tuesday - Your Challenge and a Teaching Tip

Challenge: Sign up to do something out of your comfort zone. Whether it's at your church or elsewhere, do something that might be embarrassing or nerve wracking. Be willing to try this and either fail or not be good at it in the least. Take a leap and see what happens.

Teaching Tip: Our students are forced to take these types of leaps on a regular basis. They participate in activities that might make them look silly or give presentations that have them shaking in their boots. Empathize with them, especially when you know they're trying their best. This will encourage them to learn from the experience and, hopefully, try it again.

Wednesday - Time in the Word

Ruth 1:1-17

Thursday - Prayer

Lord, You don't want us to get too comfortable down here. I believe that many times trials are allowed to come our way because You care enough to remind us that heaven is our true home. Keep us in that state of mind so that we're constantly looking to go home. Guide our hearts and minds heavenward, even as we go through the daily tasks on earth. Give us contagious, victorious faith, that others might also come to trust You with their whole hearts. This, we pray, in the name of Jesus. Amen.

Friday - Reflection

How was your week? Did you complete the challenge? What lessons did you learn? What did you see God do this week?

_____

_____

_____

Do You See What I See?

_____

_____

_____

_____

Over Before It Began

Memory Verse - "A man's heart plans his way,
but the Lord directs his steps."
Proverbs 16:9

My wife and I had been trying to see where God wanted us the next year. We both had interviews for different positions in the same month and we were praying for God to clearly show us what we should do. The positions were literally on opposite ends of the Earth so we fasted and prayed, interviewed, then fasted and prayed again.

Both of our interviews were online, with mine being was first. The interview seemed to go very well. Since I talk for a living it wasn't too stressful and I actually enjoyed the process. Then it was Sarah's turn. She doesn't talk for a living and often revisits what she has said because she's concerned it wasn't said properly or could have been misconstrued. I told her she'd be fine as I took our antsy one-year-old out for a walk so the house would be quiet.

As I was leaving, about 10 minutes prior to her interview, I heard her phone ring. I didn't think much of it until I got a call from Sarah about eight minutes later.

"Hey. It's over."

Do You See What I See?

"It's done already? Wow, that was fast."
"Yeah...they called early and caught me off guard. I don't really think it went well."

As I reassured her that she did well and she reassured me that she hadn't, I did the math quickly in my head. It was true - they had ended the interview before it was even supposed to begin! I had to admit, silently in my head of course, this wasn't the best of signs.

The results came in weeks later and they were as expected. And by expected I mean God has a great sense of humor. I was unsuccessful with my application and Sarah was successful. When Sarah told me of her acceptance I feel like God smiled and said, "I'm ordering your steps. Always have. Always will."

Oftentimes God surprises us. The two disciples on the road to Emmaus didn't know they were speaking to the risen Savior as He asked them about the conversation they were having with one another. I imagine they replied, "How haven't you heard about Jesus' death? Were you under a rock for the past three days?" Jesus, replying with a sly smile, says, "You could say that.. Tell me more." Then, step by step, Jesus leads them on a journey He had prepared long before they had a clue. A journey that would lead them to a closer walk with Him.

God is a loving parent who enjoys surprising His children with gifts. Some presents, though, are only given to those who choose to be close to His presence. Are you walking with Jesus today?

Tuesday - Your Challenge and a Teaching Tip

Challenge: Sometimes life tends to pass by too quickly. It seems like just yesterday that the school year began, now we're closer to the end than when we started. Your challenge is to try to slow down your week a bit by *praying every hour on the hour*. Say a short, silent prayer in your heart during your lesson or meeting, or spend a few minutes talking with the Lord during your break. The peace and calm that comes with completing this challenge is so wonderful that you may want to continue doing it long after this week has passed.

Teaching Tip: Quality > Quantity. When/If given the option between teaching more content or making sure the current information is understood, go with the latter. It's much better to know what you were taught than to only know you once sat in a classroom and passed a test

Wednesday - Time in the Word

Luke 24:13-35

Thursday - Prayer

Lord, before we were formed in our mother's womb You knew us. All of our faults, all the sins we would commit, all the issues we would have were well known to You. And yet You still bothered to create us. You still bothered to love us. We are grateful that You desire an even closer walk with us. Rearrange our schedules to keep You where you belong - at the start, finish, and everywhere in between - for we are nothing without You. Be our all in all so that one day we'll be in a place with You that has a beginning but no end. This is our humble prayer in Jesus' name, amen.

Friday - Reflection

How was your week? Did you complete the challenge? What lessons

Do You See What I See?

did you learn? What did you see God do this week?

_____

_____

_____

_____

_____

_____

_____

Week 23

Perhaps...

Memory Verse - "For we walk by faith, not by sight."
2 Corinthians 5:7

believe it was the same day we almost got electrocuted on the golf course. Immediately after that close encounter with lightning while holding metal clubs, we decided it was time to head home. I was the driver and the two of us, soaking wet, got into my car and started on the short but extremely windy journey. The raindrops were getting increasingly heavy and it was difficult to see, but I had driven this road hundreds of times before. I knew the road like the back of my mind. We'd be okay, right?

As we traveled at the same speed that I usually drive, I realized it wasn't smooth sailing. I glanced over at my friend next to me and he was holding on to the safety handle, not saying anything, which was very unusual. As the car veered along the road at an unsafe speed for the weather conditions, I added to his anxiety by audibly mentioning my visual condition.

"I can't see anything."

With a firmer grip and a steady tone, my friend retorted, "Perhaps you should slow down."

Do You See What I See?

A hearty laugh came from my side of the vehicle as I applied the brakes. What a simple solution to the problem - just slow down! We made it safely to our destination and to this day the word *perhaps* is a word that brings a smile to both of our faces.

Jonathan, King Saul's son, also had a life or death *perhaps* moment - this one between himself and his armour bearer. His moment, however, was not ending a needlessly crazy adventure but the exact opposite - doing something completely insane! The Israelite army was hiding in a cave from the Philistines, trying to figure out how to defeat an enemy that greatly outnumbered them. Jonathan snuck away and decided that he and his armour bearer, just the two of them, would approach the entire Philistine army by themselves. *Perhaps* God would deliver the army into their hands, was Jonathan's thought. (By the way, you need a friend like Jonathan's armour bearer.)

You, of course, know how this story ended - God honored their faith and works and took care of the rest. After using nearly all their strength to get up the mountain to the Philistines, God worked a mighty miracle for the two of them and His people.

There's no *perhaps* about it - when you step out in complete faith, He'll do the same for you!

Tuesday - Your Challenge and a Teaching Tip

Challenge: God wants you to take you on an adventure this week. Perhaps it's to slow down and take more time doing what you've done many times before. Perchance it's to do something altogether risky that seems insane to everyone around you. Take the opportunity to ask God what moment He has planned for you this week. Then faithfully walk into it.

Teaching Tip: Be solution-minded. Whether it's dealing with a student, colleague, or even a family member, try your best to not get stuck on the person, but focus on solving the problem itself. Coming up with concrete plans to fix a problem and subsequently working that plan will help keep you from being distracted and frustrated. It also gets things done much more quickly. Identify the issue, then focus on finding solutions.

Wednesday - Time in the Word

1 Samuel 14:1-23

Thursday - Prayer

You, our Lord, are pleased by those who walk by faith, for You are the Rewarder of those who diligently seek You. We often lack the faith and courage we need to do what You desire because we haven't spent enough time with You. Forgive us. Strengthen us. Move us. Perhaps we have not received the answers to prayers uttered for years as a result of us staying in the cave when we should be on the battlefield. Show us the way, Lord, and let us keep our eyes on You, for only success lies on the path on which You lead. We ask this in no other name but the name of Jesus. Amen.

Friday - Reflection

How was your week? Did you complete the challenge? What lessons did you learn? What did you see God do this week?

Do You See What I See?

_____

_____

_____

_____

_____

_____

Peanuts and Raisins

Memory Verse - "For what profit is it to a man if he gains the whole world, and loses his own soul? Or what will a man give in exchange for his soul?"
Matthew 16:26

Ninety-nine percent of the time I have some type of snack on me. As a dietary vegan, I know that there's a high probability that I'll be hungry in certain situations, so I go prepared. There's always food in my car and my bag. My sister jokes that during the time of trouble she'll find me because I'll have something to eat.

One hot Sunday morning at my church in Trench Town, Jamaica, I was waiting to tutor some students and a few young men were playing football, also known as soccer. (Only *one* of these games requires you to use your foot all the time, but I digress.) Trench Town is an extremely poor community but I've found the people to be equivalently friendly. One older man was there watching next to me and others when he said to no one in particular that he was hungry. He hadn't eaten since at least the previous day. In my bag I, of course, had some food. It was a small bag of peanuts and raisins. I gave it to him and he was very grateful. He said a quick prayer and then, as he opened the bag, looked around and offered everyone in our small group of onlookers some of his snack. I was stunned. Wasn't he hungry? There wasn't much in that bag - only one serving - why wouldn't he at least eat some before sharing with others?

I soon realized what the Trench Town community has known and practiced for years - giving to others is an investment in yourself and in your future. When I have, *we* have.

I remember a video-recorded experiment online that asked homeless people and Wall Street brokers to give away $20 that had just been handed to them. One group was willing to give, while the others just pocketed the money in their expensively tailored outfits. It was quite surprising.

The early Christians realized the importance of carrying each other's burdens. They sold their possessions so that everyone would benefit. They gave more than peanuts and raisins - they gave every earthly thing. Yet they realized, after coming in contact with the One who gave up heaven to save us, that nothing on earth should stop them from giving their all. We should endeavor to do the same, for nothing on earth is more important than the people for whom Christ died.

Tuesday - Your Challenge and Teaching Tip

Challenge: List your 3 most important material possessions. Is there something on that list that you know you wouldn't give up? If so, prayerfully ask God for a change of heart...or a way to get rid of it. The Word tells us - it's better to lose an eye or a hand than to miss out on heaven.

Teaching Tip: Teach and encourage your students to share not just material things but also information. Students who teach other students will retain the information longer, hence both students are helped in the process. Provide opportunities in class for students to do so, for life itself is a group project.

Wednesday - Time in the Word

Acts 2:38-47

Thursday - Prayer

Lord, we cannot be double-minded. There is no such thing as serving You and the things of this world simultaneously. Give us the strength to keep things in the proper perspective. Remind us anew that there's nothing that we can give in exchange for our souls. You left heaven and gave everything that we might have an eternal relationship with You. Help us to value that more than any other single thing we possess. Please also show us how we can give more to help Your people and Your cause. And once we've given, give us more so we can do it all over again. We ask these things in Jesus' name, amen.

Friday - Reflection

How was your week? Did you complete the challenge? What lessons did you learn? What did you see God do this week?

_____

_____

_____

_____

Do You See What I See?

_____

_____

_____

Week 25

Role Call

Memory Verse - "God is our refuge and strength, a very present help in trouble."
Psalm 46:1

"Here." "Present." "Aqui."

Whatever the varying responses may be throughout the year, taking attendance might be one of the most mundane activities teachers have to do on a regular basis. By the time the middle of the term comes around students who have responded to their names being called might well be present physically but their minds are in a completely different place.

Once, with about a month to go before the end of the school year, I saw it in the eyes of my students. Call it fatigue. Call it apathy. Call it whatever you wish, but I saw it and it wasn't good. They were physically present but mentally absent. I decided to try my best to get them focused but nothing I did - increasing my volume, getting excited, asking questions, telling corny jokes - worked. They had tapped out. Then I had an idea...

My friend and mentor was next door teaching his class. We taught in a trailer with a thin wooden door in between our classrooms. We had such a good rapport I decided to try something new. I walked briskly into his room and said,

"Doc, I need you to teach my class. They're unresponsive. Let's switch."
"No problem. What are you teaching?"

In less than a minute we were both teaching each others' classes. Even though we hadn't known each others' lessons for that period, neither one of us missed a beat. Predictably, with a "new" teacher, the students perked up and, albeit initially confused, ended up learning more than they expected during that period. Switching roles had worked wonderfully.

Psalm 46:1 is a verse that left me scratching my head for a long time. I know what it means to be present, but what does it mean to be *very* present? Reading through how God saved His people by taking them through the Red Sea on dry ground, I realized that you can be present but not seen and not felt. You can be present but not fully attentive. God tells us that, yes, He will never leave us nor forsake us so He is always there. But when the troublesome times come, when the trials are at their worst, He'll appear in ways that He hasn't before. His status on the roll hasn't changed - He's still present - yet His role has. He's promising to be seen, to be felt, and to give You His undivided attention. A very present Help indeed!

Tuesday - Your Challenge and a Teaching Tip

Challenge: Within your realm of teaching expertise and with someone with whom you are comfortable, switch classes for a session. You'll definitely want to plan this in advance more than I did. Just hearing another voice talking and teaching can energize the students and invigorate teachers. Start planning it this week, especially if your students' attentiveness is waning.

Teaching Tip: After you've learned the students names and taking attendance becomes routine, it's easier to count the number of students in the class then subtract that from the total on the roster. Then ask those present to tell you who's missing that day. This will not only lessen the amount of time dedicated to this task but it can "wake up" a few students as they check for their classmates.

Wednesday - Time in the Word

Exodus 14:10-31

Thursday - Prayer

You, Lord, completed the quintessential role-reversal when You came down to earth as a man that we might be able to experience eternal life. Words are neither sufficient to comprehend or appreciate what You've done for us. We simply say thank You and ask for You to help us develop in our roles as Christians. Help us to empathize with the plights of others and assist as You desire. Move us out of our comfort zones that lives might be changed not just for time but for eternity. Ultimately, help us to let them know that, because of Your role as sacrificial Lamb, we are certain that when the roll is called up yonder we can all be there. Thank You, in Jesus' name. Amen.

Friday - Reflection

How was your week? Did you complete the challenge? What lessons did you learn? What did you see God do this week?

Do You See What I See?

_____

_____

_____

_____

_____

_____

Content Under Pressure

Memory Verse - "I know how to be abased, and I know how to abound. Everywhere and in all things I have learned both to be full and to be hungry, both to abound and to suffer need. I can do all things through Christ who strengthens me."
Philippians 4:12-13

From Keith "Cateyes" Kinsey in Atlanta to Joseph in Kingston to John in Melbourne, I enjoy conversing with people who are homeless. I do enjoy donating to causes associated with helping them, but I find that a conversation can be quite helpful to their humanity...and mine too.

The stories I've heard from these three, and many others, have run the full gamut of emotion. From gut-wrenching to hysterical, the stories they shared, including how they ended up on the streets, were always fascinating. Keith worked on a construction site when a piece of machinery fell on his back and he was unable to work. He gave the settlement money to his children to go to school and tried his best from there on out. Joseph wasn't mentally well and, sadly, recently passed away.

Of the three, John is the most unique. It seems that he actually wants to be homeless. He has his daily routine, which includes getting two meals from a local community center and reading many books. He has family nearby but likes to sleep on a bench near the trolley tracks. Every time I ask if he needs anything at all, he'll politely say no. Does he want to come over for a meal? No, thanks. Let's go out to eat? No, he's okay. A round of golf? He still has his 6 iron but says he's too old for a full round now. He's a recluse and I had to trick him in order to find out his birthday. When I showed up with a cake and candles on December 5th to celebrate his 84th birthday, he enjoyed it but tried his best to recall how I'd gotten that information out of him. John is the most content homeless person, and probably one of the most content people, I've ever met.

Paul tells us in many of his writings how material things have little to do with being content. He once had much and later had almost nothing. He'd been honored by men and he'd been abused, beaten, and stoned by them as well. Throughout it all, throughout all the pressures of life, Paul remained content. Why? It could only be because he kept his eyes fixed on Jesus.

Would you be able to be content through all of that? Even as you try to progress in your career and otherwise, are you content with what you have now? It's only possible if we're similarly focused on Christ.

Tuesday - Your Challenge and a Teaching Tip

Challenge: The challenge this week is to fast and pray during the school day. Unless physically unable, spend the time you usually would eat at work in prayer. (Feel free to choose something else from which to fast if you can't skip out on meals). Gauge your level of contentment at the end of each school day by doing a short, written comparison between how you feel physically, emotionally, and spiritually everyday.

Teaching Tip: To keep your sanity (and maybe your job), you may want to wait 24 hours before responding to disrespectful/unprofessional emails from parents, students, or administrators. Also, you may simply reply that you would like to set up a meeting, in person or on the phone, to discuss the issues. Generally speaking, when some time has been allotted for all parties to cool down, these discussions are much more productive.

Wednesday - Time in the Word

2 Corinthians 11:22-30

Thursday - Prayer

As You know well, Lord, there are some days where being content doesn't seem possible. Whether it's people getting on our nerves, circumstances beyond our control, or sins that beset us, we often can't see how contentment is a plausible consideration. Yet You tell us when these things begin to happen that we need to look up and lift up our heads for our redemption is near. And because we know this, we can be content and we can have joy. We don't rejoice for all things but we can rejoice in all things, knowing that You will never leave us. Thank You for Your promises and Your love. Guide us daily to live like You want us to - with heaven in view. This we pray in Jesus' name, amen.

Friday - Reflection

How was your week? Did you complete the challenge? What lessons did you learn? What did you see God do this week?

_____

_____

Do You See What I See?

_____

_____

_____

_____

_____

Week 27

Speak Up

Memory Verse - "A man who has friends must himself be friendly, but there is a friend who sticks closer than a brother."
Proverbs 18:24

Disclaimer: This is a true story. Not to say that the others aren't, but, well, this one might seem far-fetched.

I attended and graduated from Morehouse College (where Robert Smith, Jr. gave maybe the greatest commencement speech ever - he funded the student loans of all the graduates). I used to be pretty quiet and reclusive so I didn't talk to many people, but I did have some good friends. One afternoon I spotted one of my loud and gregarious classmates just before the cafeteria opened. As we met on the path, I could tell he was quite upset. I decided to ask him what was happening...

"Hey, what's going on? Don't you have class now?"
"Man, I got kicked out!"
"What happened?!"
"I was in Dr. Oyedeji's class, sitting in the front and he was talkin' but I couldn't understand what he was sayin'," he said as he shook his head.

My eyes got wide as this professor is known to be very strict and has a military-type classroom atmosphere. My friend continued...

Do You See What I See?

"So I said, 'Hey, Doc. Can you speak English?' He says, 'I am speaking perfect English.' I said, 'No you ain't! 'Cause if you was I could understand what you was sayin'!'"

I'm not certain, but I believe my mouth dropped completely open in disbelief. My friend wasn't finished. Dr. Oyedeji had a question for him...

"'What is your name?'
'My name Ephraim.'
'Get out!'"

As Ephraim stormed off to his door room, I couldn't help but laugh. He had to have known that he would get kicked out if he acted like that in front of any professor, but especially Dr. Oyedeji. He got what he deserved - including a one-week ban from the class.

When the violently demon-possessed man came into contact with Jesus, the forces of evil must similarly have known that they would be kicked out by the Teacher for acting up. Jesus, too, asked them their name and kicked them out. Their ban, however, was permanent. Sometimes God allows the enemy to come together, as Legion had, so He can fast-track their defeat.

It's great to have a friend whom you know will speak up when the going gets tough. The one who will step in if anyone in your group of friends is disrespected or if things start to get serious. Ephraim, in his own way, would be that friend. But there is a Friend who sticks closer than a brother. One who will always have Your back. I'm thankful that Jesus speaks up for us - not just to demons, but, more importantly, to His Father. Return the favor - speak up for Him today.

Tuesday - Your Challenge and a Teaching Tip

Challenge: Be an advocate for students who need someone to speak on their behalf. Having a voice is powerful and many students, unfortunately, aren't heard or represented. The challenge this week is to seek to identify a student or group, within the school or outside, that you can lend your voice to support. Speak up!

Teaching Tip: Advocating for students includes giving them the means to find their own voice. As often as feasible, allow your students to make presentations, ask and answer questions, and give speeches. Being able to properly communicate one's thoughts, without being defensive and staying on subject, is an indispensable skill to have in the 21st century.

Wednesday - Time in the Word

Mark 5:1-15

Thursday - Prayer

Lord, we thank You for the conversation that the Trinity has within Itself. We thank You for advocating and interceding for us, even as the accuser of the brethren tries his best to derail Your plans for our lives. We are unworthy to approach Your throne of grace, but since You have made us worthy, we come. Give us the strength to speak for those who have no voice. Give us the fortitude and the stamina to continue to pray for those who do not pray but need You more than anything. Give us more of You. Speak to us and through us is our prayer today in Jesus' name. Amen.

Do You See What I See?

Friday - Reflection

How was your week? Did you complete the challenge? What lessons did you learn? What did you see God do this week?

_____

_____

_____

_____

_____

_____

_____

Who Are You?

Memory Verse - "Therefore, if anyone is in Christ, he is a new creation; old things have passed away; behold, all things have become new."
2 Corinthians 5:17

I try my best to be on time but inevitably I'll arrive late to some events. Regardless of what time I arrive, I try to get a good seat. I've found that if you arrive just late enough you can find a seat close to or in the section marked "Reserved" and no one will ask you to move. In order to do so there are usually a few things you must know and do. (I'm giving away these tips since having a toddler prohibits me from using them.) First, enter dressed properly and with confidence. What you wear needs to match the attire for the program, but the closer you are to being overdressed the better. Second, act like you are in charge and walk with your chin up. Don't look for or be afraid to make eye contact as you go forward. Lastly, you must be prepared to be humbled. Hope for the best, plan for the worst.

I've been successful in these endeavors for quite some time. At a choral and orchestral concert in Jamaica a few years ago, I tried to see if such a plan would work internationally. It did. I arrived just before the concert started and all the dignitaries had already been seated. I found myself in the second row of the reserved section.

111

Do You See What I See?

The concert was delightful. During a break, however, the gentleman next to me turned and introduced himself. In the most authentic French accent you can imagine he said,

"Good evening. I am the French Ambassador. And you are?"

I froze. Who was I? I immediately knew neither my name nor my profession was of any importance. I had to come up with something. Keeping my composure, I replied with the truth of my status. In that moment I realized the only thing that mattered was my relationship with the one in charge.

"Good evening. My brother-in-law is the Director and Composer tonight." (Thanks, Andrew!)

In the book of Acts, there are seven sons of Sceva who took it upon themselves to try to exorcise a demon from a man. Unfortunately, they didn't have a relationship with the One in charge. They tried using His name but that wasn't good enough. The demon said to them, "Jesus I know, and Paul I know, but who are you?" What a frightening scene it must have been as the demon beat all seven of them out of their clothes!

The question, though, still remains - who are you? I'm not asking for your name, neither am I asking for your position or where you went to school. Who are you? It's an existential question we all need to answer. Ultimately, it's a question that can only be properly answered in light of your relationship with Jesus Christ.

Tuesday - Your Challenge and a Teaching Tip

Challenge: When we enter into a loving relationship with God He gives us a gift. If you haven't done so recently, find a spiritual gifts inventory online and find out which gift(s) God has given you. It may not be perfect but it's a start to finding out who Christ has called you to be. You cannot leave it there though. Once you know what your gifts are you must use them. Whether it's within your local church or outside in the community, use the gift(s) with which Christ has blessed you. Soon you may be blessed with even more!

Teaching Tip: Take your appearance seriously. For students who wear uniforms to school, it's been said that their scores on exams given outside of regular school hours are higher when they put on their uniforms. It's believed that their outfits help to get their minds in the correct framework for the exams. In the same way, we need to dress for success, even if it's not required by your school. With impressionable minds in front of us everyday, make it a point to dress well, that students may be certain that you take your job and this profession seriously.

Wednesday - Time in the Word

Acts 19:11-20

Thursday - Prayer

Thank You, Lord, for defining us. We exist only by Your creative power and we can only know who we truly are through a relationship with You. You showed us how important we are through Your life-giving sacrifice on Calvary. You continue to demonstrate Your love as You prepare a place and have a new name awaiting each of us. We cannot thank You enough. As we go through our daily trials and tribulations, keep us focused on who we are in Your eyes. Ensure that our perspective might always be heavenward, even as we try to do the most earthly good. We pray this in Jesus' name, amen.

Friday - Reflection

How was your week? Did you complete the challenge? What lessons did you learn? What did you see God do this week?

_____

_____

_____

_____

_____

_____

_____

Reclaiming My Time

Memory Verse - "But the end of all things is at hand; therefore be serious and watchful in your prayers."
1 Peter 4:7

Does that have any redeeming value?"

My mother used a wonderful, mind-torturing strategy on me when she found me watching any TV show that was questionable for my age. As she passed by, she would simply ask that question then walk away without waiting for a response...or excuses. I remember watching those shows as a teenager and I thought many were quite comical. I knew they were a little raunchy for my age and most of the jokes and topics weren't ones a Christian should share with anyone else, but it was funny and I didn't think it was *too* bad.

But now I'm stuck in a dilemma. I can't get that question out of my head. Do I continue watching? I mean, my mom didn't explicitly tell me to stop so really I could just finish this show and then go find something valuable to do. Somehow though, as I tried to continue watching, the jokes were no longer as funny and my mind kept going back to the question. Mission accomplished, Mommy.

Some lessons last a lifetime. A few years ago my wife and I turned off our cable. It wasn't the financial cost but the mental cost that led us to such a choice. It was a great decision. I'm not sure how many hours we've saved, but our heads are no longer cluttered by what others, most of whom have no respect for God, are trying to put into our minds via the TV. We've reclaimed our time.

On a rare occasion (aka when Joshua falls asleep early), we'll watch a movie together - usually a historical documentary. Recently we paid to rent what I thought was such a film. A few moments in I realized this wasn't the type of cinema I expected nor wanted to watch. As egregious violence and the breaking of many commandments, including taking the Lord's name in vain, occurred incessantly before us, we had a calculation to make. Yes, we had already paid for it. There were no refunds and I have a real disdain for wasting money. But was it worth it? We wouldn't have enough time to decide on another movie and we didn't know when we would get another opportunity like this. What should we do?

We turned it off.

Joshua (the Bible character) was literally able to reclaim time when the sun stood still as he routed the enemies of God's people. The forces of evil had come together to attack, but Joshua was unafraid since he had God on his side. He, wanting the complete victory God had promised, made time stop.

Similarly, Jesus wants to completely remove the enemies that have come together to steal your time and attention away from what's important. Will you let Him? It has taken years, but I've decided that what I allow to enter my mind is important. I've learned to reclaim my time. I encourage you to take the time to do the same.

Tuesday - Your Challenge and a Teaching Tip

Challenge: There's a difference between entertainment and recreation. The former involves being mostly sedentary, both physically and mentally, while the latter stimulates both - it re-creates (*Education*, p. 208). Take stock of your extracurriculars and, for this entire week (including the weekend), replace the things that are entertaining with things that are recreational.

Teaching Tip: It's been said that we shouldn't sweat the small stuff and that's true - it takes too much of our time and adds unnecessary stress. However, if a student's behavior is poor and it affects other students to the point where they're behaving similarly, you must react appropriately to have the behavior cease. Gauging and stopping these behaviors from the beginning can be crucial to having a motivated and successful classroom.

Wednesday - Time in the Word

Joshua 10:1-15

Thursday - Prayer

Lord, the devil tries his utmost best to keep us from spending quality time with You. He works through the distractions and excuses that we make, trying to have us believe things won't be so bad or won't make a lasting impression. Yet by beholding we are changed. As the end is near, help us to realize how important the little things are, for the devil just wants an inch that he might fully take over soon thereafter. We ask that You refresh and renew our minds that we might be able to walk the straight and narrow path with Your leading and guidance. In truth, things that may be safe for others to do may not be for us. Give us the wherewithal to distinguish and the strength to do what we need to do. We thank You in advance for Your power that we can access to accomplish this, in Jesus' name. Amen.

Friday - Reflection

How was your week? Did you complete the challenge? What lessons did you learn? What did you see God do this week?

_____

_____

_____

_____

_____

_____

_____

Week 30

What Are You Doing?

Memory Verse - "His lord said to him, 'Well done, good and faithful servant; you have been faithful over a few things, I will make you ruler over many things. Enter into the joy of your lord.'"
Matthew 25:23

Our school took a trip from the East coast of the United States to the European cities of Paris, London, and Madrid. For me it ended up being more of a work trip than a vacation as the teachers were responsible for the safety and well-being of more than 40 high schoolers. We had had a good and mostly uneventful journey as we boarded the train for an overnight ride from Paris to Madrid.

Just before we alighted from the bus to get onto the train, our tour guide made sure he had everyone's attention. He told an elaborate story of a young girl who had gotten off the train and was left at a station. It took more than two days and a lot of money for her family to find her. The moral of the story - don't get off the train. He had the entire bus repeat that phrase several times before we left.

I figure you know where this story is headed. Nevertheless, I'll share the details. We were running late but we made it just before the train was to pull off. I was helping everyone get their luggage onboard and we were close to finishing. A freshman male was last and, as I turned away from him to put on his bag I heard him say, "I have to go to the bathroom." With that, he started to take a step off the train. My head whipped around and I grabbed the back of his jacket with one hand and yanked him back up. His foot never touched the ground outside the train.

"What are you doing?!?" I asked after I'd spun him around and held his arms firmly. My eyes were locked on his as I stared at him in utter disbelief. I couldn't understand why he had unequivocally disregarded what he had just heard on the bus. (For the record, the bathroom he was looking for was over 800 meters away in a convenience store where he would have had to purchase something in order to use their facility. The nearest bathroom was, of course, on the train - less than a meter from where we stood.)

Many people make bad decisions in times of crisis. This is why we have drills of all types in our schools. Archilochus, a Greek poet, is attributed with an appropriate quote for such times, said, "You don't rise to the occasion. You sink to your level of training" (Frank, 2016).

Unfortunately, King Saul's training was like my student's - a command was stated plainly to him but never internalized. Saul had explicit instructions to wait on the Lord and His prophet Samuel. However, when things got a little dicey and his patience wore thin, we got to see who Saul truly was at his core. His actions answered the question atop this devotion - Saul was a man who trusted himself more than anyone else. Now, in this time of crisis, he was simply showing everyone else.

Do your attitude and actions change when times get tough? How do you react when you've been given a command to which you don't want to adhere? Often God builds our characters in times like these. Take a few moments to figure out your triggers. Have a song or scripture ready to keep you close to God for when they start to occur.

Tuesday - Your Challenge and a Teaching Tip

Challenge: Obedience is better than sacrifice. Adhering to what God says to do is better than having to ask for forgiveness after the deed has been done. Yet it's our daily habits, what we do with the little things, that determine our character and ultimately our eternal destiny. The challenge this week is for those who drive. It's a difficult one. All week, no matter how late you may be, don't drive above the speed limit. As we want our students to be obedient to authority, we should also do the same. Try it out and see. (Caution - I previously gave this challenge and at least one person who ignored it got a big ticket!)

For those who don't drive, choose a rule that you break easily without consequence. Whether it's littering, downloading something illegally, or something else, refrain from it completely this week (including using whatever you may have obtained online illegally).

Teaching Tip: Unfortunately, too many students don't use their time wisely as they prepare for tests and exams. This may lead to them to break the rules and try to cheat their way to a higher score. One of the telltale signs of a student cheating is if he/she makes eye contact with you more than once during the test. At that point you should closely inspect their surroundings to see if the student is accessing any unauthorized material.

Wednesday - Time in the Word

1 Samuel 15:10-26

Do You See What I See?

Thursday - Prayer

Lord, we don't like the word "obey." It signifies a lack of control and we as educators like when we're in control. From our youth we've realized that it's difficult being obedient to authority. Yet we simultaneously know that adherence to Your rules is what's best for us. It's much better to listen the first time and do the right thing than to need to apologize and pay the consequences. We ask for the courage to let You lead. We ask for the faith to trust You every step. We ask for Your power and peace to be true disciples. And we thank You in Jesus' name, amen.

Friday - Reflection

How was your week? Did you complete the challenge? What lessons did you learn? What did you see God do this week?

_____

_____

_____

_____

_____

_____

_____

Week 31

Who's the Boss?

Memory Verse - "And if it seems evil to you to serve the Lord, choose for yourselves this day whom you will serve, whether the gods which your fathers served that were on the other side of the River, or the gods of the Amorites, in whose land you dwell. But as for me and my house, we will serve the Lord."
Joshua 24:15

I like being in charge. You may share the same sentiment. If something goes wrong I'd rather it be my fault than anyone else's. For example, I cut my own hair. If I mess it up it's ok, but if I pay someone and they mess it up I'll be upset - with myself.

One of my favorite movie scenes is from *Remember the Titans* (2000). The two biggest personalities are the team captain, who is white, and his roommate, the black teammate he needs the most. The movie is set during a time of recent school desegregation in the US and these two football players don't get along. Finally they decide to hash things out, with no holds barred. The last few lines of the conversation go something like this:

WG   "You're leavin' your teammates out to dry, me in particular!"

BG   "I'm supposed to wear myself out for the team? What team?! Naw, I'm gonna go out there and I'm gonna to get mine."

Do You See What I See?

WG   "Man, that's the worst attitude I've ever heard."

BG   (pregnant pause, then looking his teammate in the eye) "Attitude reflects leadership, captain."

That last line has resonated with me since I first heard it. Leadership is truly important. Those who are supposed to follow are greatly affected by the attitude and psyche of their leader.

No matter how great a leader may be, there will be disagreements. I've been blessed to have had very competent principals throughout my teaching career. More than that, I've been able to argue, fuss, and fight with them behind closed doors, but leave with a smile, a handshake and a united message. Your boss(es) may be fantastic or fantastically incompetent. However, that's not the query. The question isn't who's the Boss, for God unquestionably has that title. The question really is, who's *your* boss?

Despite all the challenges he faced, most of his own making, Jacob never forgot Who was in charge. The biggest test of his life was in front of him. His life was at stake and he knew he deserved to die at his brother's hand. Yet, in this time of times, he resorted to his God. And from then on he let *the* Boss be *his* Boss. It saved his life and started him on a journey as a leader of God's people.

I dare say, no matter what kind of leader you're under, your attitude reflects whom you've chosen to follow - either God or yourself. When things go wrong, and they will, do you roll your eyes and complain? Do you talk about your leaders behind their backs? Or do you talk about them on your knees? Who do you talk to first when you don't like a decision that's been made or how something was done? Regardless of what the chain of command is stated to be at your job, your reaction to setbacks shows whom you've decided to let lead. Choose well.

Tuesday - Your Challenge and a Teaching Tip

Challenge: Give your boss a compliment this week. Whether by email, handwritten note, or in a one-on-one conversation, find something that your boss does well and let her or him know about it and that you appreciate it. This can be especially tough with bosses who have gaps in their leadership, but speak this positive truth in love to them, in Jesus' name.

Teaching Tip: Be cognizant and inclusive of multiple perspectives and cultures when you teach. Often times our textbooks have been written by the "winners" who speak with the voice of the majority. Allow your students to hear the other side(s) of the story, for some who have been called heroes are elsewhere known as villains. This will hopefully allow everyone to empathize with others and start conversations that open eyes and hearts.

Wednesday - Time in the Word

Genesis 32:22-33:4

Thursday - Prayer

Lord, it's amazing that with Your power and sovereignty You still allow us to choose who we want to be our leader. It's easy to say that we are Your servants but it's difficult to do. Help us this day to choose to serve You totally, that our homes and our hearts might be places where Your Spirit thrives. Even more than that, give us the power to make this choice daily, so that as Your employees we will receive the full benefits of working in Your vineyard. This we pray in the name of our Lord and

Do You See What I See?

Savior, Jesus Christ. Amen.

Friday - Reflection

How was your week? Did you complete the challenge? What lessons did you learn? What did you see God do this week?

_____

_____

_____

_____

_____

_____

_____

Incomplete

Memory Verse - "Being confident of this very thing, that He who has begun a good work in you will complete it until the day of Jesus Christ."
Philippians 1:6

My uncle, Michael Jones Sr., once said that educators must be lifelong learners. I knew I wanted to be a teacher from early on and continually learning new things is truly fundamental to doing so. When I was in my mid-teens I figured I needed to learn a few things outside the classroom. The list included how to cook, construct, and fix a car - and so I did. (For the record, this was all before YouTube videos existed!)

One other thing I wanted to do was to be able to use my left hand almost as well as I use my right. Throwing a ball with my off-hand always looked terrible and never went where I wanted. Since I enjoyed playing basketball, baseball, and American football, I sometimes needed my left hand. I decided enough was enough and went to work to try to fix this "issue."

It takes more work than you would think to throw things well with your weak hand. (Give it a shot and see.) After months of practice I had taught my muscles a new thing or two and my left hand was actually getting better than my right. But you never know if it really works until you're pressed up against it.

It became the best pass I ever threw in an American football game. It was our annual Thanksgiving Day football game and I was playing quarterback. We wore no pads and it was full tackle. This means the play isn't over until the player with the ball is either on the ground or out of bounds, or if a forward pass isn't caught. (Yes, I know. There's a reason for protective gear. But let's continue...)

The game was close and we had the ball. The defense was running toward me from my right so I dashed to my left. To throw the ball with my right hand as I ran left would require me to stop and turn. I would've been knocked to the ground before any of that could've happened. What could I do? As they say, the way you practice is the way you play. I put the ball in my left hand and threw it to an open teammate just before a defender threw me to the ground. I watched as a perfect spiral darted towards my teammate. Suddenly a hand came out of nowhere and knocked the ball to the ground. Incomplete. As I dusted myself off, I had a huge grin on my face. I thought to myself, "It worked! What a great throw!"

I threw for about five touchdowns that game (all with my right hand) and we ended up winning easily. Yet the pass I remember the most was one that never got to it's intended recipient.

There's a certain joy that happens during the process towards success. Yes, there are failures. There will absolutely be defeats and devastating moments. Still, once that sliver of light shines through, there follows a joy that nothing else can match.

I think Tamar felt incomplete for many years. Her husband died and she didn't have any children. She was supposed to, by law, have a child by one of her brothers-in-law. They, to say it politically correctly, didn't completely fulfill their end of the bargain. And so Tamar was left incomplete. Her father-in-law, Judah, should have done better but he betrayed her as well. Ultimately, she took matters into her own hands and ended up getting pregnant by Judah. She nearly lost her life in the process, but I believe she finally started to feel complete.

Yet God wasn't done with her story. In the first chapter of the book of Matthew you'll find that Tamar is in the lineage of, wait for it, Jesus Christ! Sometimes, during the process things become tearfully cloudy. In the midst of those times remember that God isn't finished with you yet. He who began a good work in you will be faithful to *complete* it.

Tuesday - Your Challenge and a Teaching Tip

Challenge: As Psalm 1 states, evening and morning worship is important. This week make it a point to set time aside in the morning *and* evening to worship God. Plan it well and, unless there's an emergency, keep that time as sacred.

Teaching Tip: Recognizing that each child has a different beginning and ending to her or his story can remind us how important, or not, we can be to our students. Know that we play a crucial role in each student's development, but that our role pales in comparison to the Author and Creator of life. Keep your perspective fixed on who God needs and requires you to be in each of their lives. This is a great guide not just for your teaching practice but also for all your interactions.

Wednesday - Time in the Word

Genesis 38:1-26

Do You See What I See?

Thursday - Prayer

Lord, we all like a good story. As educators, we enjoy seeing the end of the process. However, sometimes we need to pause in the midst and contemplate what You want us to learn. Sometimes the journey is indeed the destination and we thank You for being our GPS. Even if we don't know where we are headed today, please direct us so that someone might be empowered and motivated to follow us to Your throne of peace and love. And once there, help us never to leave. We ask all this in Jesus' name, amen.

Friday - Reflection

How was your week? Did you complete the challenge? What lessons did you learn? What did you see God do this week?

_____

_____

_____

_____

_____

_____

_____

Week 33

No Need for Speed

Memory Verse - "Wait on the Lord; Be of good courage, and He shall strengthen your heart; Wait, I say, on the Lord!"
Psalm 27:14

Have you ever driven in a car without brakes? No, that isn't a trick question. My first car was a 1989 Volkswagen Jetta. I had worked to buy this car before my junior year in college and I was very proud to be a car owner.

I picked up the Jetta from Washington, D.C., intending to drive the three hours home to Philadelphia. The seller told me about the nice interior and the brand new wheels. Unfortunately he forgot to tell me the brakes weren't good. As I was driving, I noticed that no matter how hard I tried, the car wouldn't slow down any faster than it had when I applied initial pressure to the brakes. Yes, the car had brakes. They just weren't good. At one point, I ended up having to veer into a gas station to avoid hitting the car in front of me.

The big issue was that in a couple of days I was planning to drive with my mom in my "new" car to Atlanta, which is about 14 hours away. By the time we were scheduled to leave I had gotten used to how far ahead of time I needed to push the brake pedal in order to stop. I also knew the maximum speed I could go in order to be safe on the highways. (Cruise control is a wonderful invention.) My mom, however, knew none of this. I hadn't told her because I wasn't expecting her to drive.

Did you know that 14 hours is a long time to be behind the wheel? I soon realized I needed a, well, break. We stopped on the side of the highway and my mom took over the driving. She drives much faster than I do. As soon as she hit the accelerator I knew sleep was no longer an option for me. As we were getting off the highway onto an inclined ramp to stop for gas, I told my mom to hit the brakes. She ignored me, probably thinking she had plenty of time. Since I figured our lives were at stake, I repeated it a few times, increasing the cadence and intensity of my voice each time. Finally she hit the breaks - but I knew it was too late. The Jetta calmly flew through the stop sign and finally came to rest in the middle of the intersection. Thank God no cars were coming in either direction.

"You know, your brakes aren't good."

Yes, Mommy. I know. But God is!

Jesus took a break from vocally responding to the Pharisees by bending down and writing in the sand. The woman's accusers wanted immediate "justice" and sentencing, but the Lord had other plans. As He did at creation, He stooped down and shifted some dirt to make life. This time, as He wrote the punishable-by-death sins of the men condemning her, He saved Mary. There was no rush in Him, the Author of time, for in that moment her eternal life was at stake.

With so many things to do, sometimes we end up rushing through life. Even when we try to slow down something else forces us back into the fast lane. Be intentional this week. Guard your time well and slow down a bit, especially since lives are in the balance.

Tuesday - Your Challenge and a Teaching Tip

Challenge: Many times in life we wish we could start over. We would do some things differently if we were given the chance. This week, surprise someone in your life with a do-over. It may be that you allow your students to take an alternate exam that replaces a bad one, or that you forget an offense against you. Seek the opportunity to turn back the clock and give someone a second chance.

Teaching Tip: Having enough time to complete an exam is imperative for students to have and keep their confidence in a subject. A belief by students that an assessment did not allow them to demonstrate their full knowledge may project onto the teacher, the class, and even school itself. It may manifest in myriad ways, including bad behavior and resentment. Be very mindful that your exams have sufficient time to be completed.

Wednesday - Time for the Word

John 8:2-11

Thursday - Prayer

Lord, the number of second chances we've received has outnumbered the prescribed 70 times 7 to the nth degree. Yet this is precisely what You require of us. Give us hearts willing to forgive. Since we're too often moving too fast, slow us down a bit this week, even today, that we might glimpse You more closely. Help us to see more clearly how You're working in our lives. Thank You for the time You've given us. Allow us to use it wisely that You might be honored and glorified through our interactions and activities. We pray this in Jesus' name. Amen.

Friday - Reflection

How was your week? Did you complete the challenge? What lessons did you learn? What did you see God do this week?

_____

_____

_____

_____

_____

_____

_____

Week 34

Exposed

Memory Verse - "And you shall know the truth, and the truth shall make you free."
John 8:32

ndrew was celebrating his 10th birthday when the unthinkable happened. He has just gotten into the car and was heading home. He was sitting in the backseat after leaving a restaurant and he could no longer hold his tongue. Something must be said.

"Dad, you know you left money on the table at the restaurant?!"

My eyes squinted in confusion. Had I? Did I need to turn around? Then it clicked.

"Oh! Son, that's called a tip! You leave that for the servers." I said as a smile came across my face.

A few new things occurred for Andrew that night. He had just been to his first supermarket and he learned about tipping. I could almost hear his brain churning to comprehend why a passerby wouldn't come after us, take the money off the table and run. I had taken for granted the fact that he, having lived well below the poverty line all of his life, hadn't been exposed to much outside of his community.

Having exposure to different norms, cultures, and styles can reduce stereotypes, correct false assumptions, and increase open-mindedness. Being exposed to the wrong things leads to a less than optimal functioning of the mind and soul. (To be sure, anyone who says we should allow ourselves or our loved ones a dose of evil every so often should know that evil is around every corner. We need not access it intentionally. (*The Adventist Home*, p. 13).)

If your camera's exposure settings are incorrect your pictures will be dreadful. The same is true regarding our exposure. The devil can transform himself into an angel of light, and only darkness and despair are seen there. However, exposure to the Light will have unparalleled illumination.

In the book of John we see a woman at a well whose life had been exposed. Even at midday she was living in darkness. Though she went to the well when the sun was at its apex, she still couldn't see past her problems. But when the Son broke through her facade and hardened heart, she was set free - for whom the Son sets free is free indeed.

Here's a tip - you can't hide from Jesus, for He still illuminates the world. Let Him totally in and He'll bring you out of darkness into His marvelous light.

Tuesday - Your Challenge and a Teaching Tip

Challenge: Being exposed to some "lights" can actually diminish our potential. The challenge this week is with a literal light that can be addictive. For the next seven days don't use your phone for the first 15 minutes after you wake up or for the last 30 before you get into bed. Save this time to clear your mind and talk with Jesus.

Teaching Tip: It's difficult dealing with students who are in conflict with each other. It's important that you're sure to hear both sides of the story before making a decision. The first person you hear usually seems accurate, but often it's not the full account of what occurred. Take time to listen before adjudicating.

Wednesday - Time in the Word

John 4:6-26

Thursday - Prayer

This little light of mine, I'm gonna let it shine. Let it shine 'til Jesus comes, I'm gonna let it shine. Lord, allow Your light to shine through us. Allow those who are exposed to us to be sure to know that we have been with You. Let the light of Your glory fill us so much that we, like Moses, might be radiant. Let what develops from this relationship with You remove all darkness, that we might fully reflect Your image. This is our prayer, in Jesus' name. Amen.

Friday - Reflection

How was your week? Did you complete the challenge? What lessons did you learn? What did you see God do this week?

_____

_____

_____

_____

Do You See What I See?

_____

_____

_____

None Can Compare

Memory Verse - "For the Lord does not see as man sees; for man looks at the outward appearance, but the Lord looks at the heart."
1 Samuel 16:7

"Y̲ou're not doing it right."

It's bad enough that the little boy had continually disrupted camp with his poor behavior. Now he was telling me that I was disciplining his incorrectly. The nerve, the temerity, the unmitigated gall of this precocious young man! Nevermind that he was correct...

The previous day another leader had taken him for a long, tough-love, walk around the camp grounds. It was clear that the young man was acting out due to issues that had nothing to do with being at our five-week overnight camp, but he was still ours to manage. Unfortunately, the following day that leader was elsewhere when the bad behavior began again. I had only seen from afar what had been done, but I figured it was worth trying to recreate. We started to walk around the campus and I really had no clue what I was doing besides getting exercise and talking to him about his likes and dislikes. That's when he told me, in no uncertain terms, that I needed a better strategy.

It was a humbling experience, even as I mumbled to the boy that I wasn't trying to do exactly what the other camp leader had done. He had compared me to someone else who had done a better job than I was doing. What made it worse was that I was comparing myself as well. This is a classic fault of humanity, and Christianity in particular. We look at others and think we either can't measure up to or that we're much better than others. God created you uniquely to do things that no one else can. What you do and how you do it, if properly utilizing the gifts God has given, will produce an outcome that would not occur otherwise.

Sarai doubled-checked her birth certificate and then looked up to see her young handmaiden. "Surely," Sarai must have thought, "Hagar is a better option to provide a child for my husband. She's young, fertile and verile. I'm old and well past my prime. There's no comparison. Let me tell Abram what he should do..."

In short order Sarai regretted her decision. She had not consulted with the Lord because she was too busy looking at someone else. God had a specific plan to do something miraculous for and through her, and He was still able to do so. However, the consequences of her not looking to Him first were dire and long-lasting.

We need to learn from Sarai's story and keep our focus on who God wants us to be. For surely, no one can compare to Him, and nothing can compare to the plan He has for your life.

Tuesday - Your Challenge and a Teaching Tip

Challenge: Think of the individual at your school who either has the most difficult job or who works the longest hours and whose position is generally considered less prominent than yours. It may be the custodian, nurse, food service provider, or security guard. Whomever it may be, find them and thank them for their service to the school. Doing so will hopefully make their day and give them a nice story to tell when they get home.

Teaching Tip: Don't compare students to each other. You may highlight a student's *positive* behavior to the class, but in a one-on-one conversation do not bring up how well other students are doing in comparison. Never say, "You should be more like _____" or "Why can't you act like _____?" Push students to be their best selves, not duplicates of others.

Wednesday - Time in the Word

Genesis 16:1-6, 17:15-19

Thursday - Prayer

Lord, we thank You for being the God who creates each snowflake with a different design and no zebra to have the same stripes. We appreciate the uniqueness of each person You've created, even if they share the same DNA. We are more than grateful that You care enough about each of us to send Your only Son to become like us that we might be saved. None can compare to You. And because You are the standard, please help us not to compare ourselves to others, for better or for worse. Give us the confidence to be who You've designed us to be and to allow those in our care to do the same. We love You and we thank You, in Jesus' name. Amen.

Friday - Reflection

How was your week? Did you complete the challenge? What lessons did you learn? What did you see God do this week?

Do You See What I See?

_____

_____

_____

_____

_____

_____

Week 36

The Bored Room

Memory Verse - "For the word of God is living and powerful, and sharper than any two-edged sword, piercing even to the division of soul and spirit, and of joints and marrow, and is a discerner of the thoughts and intents of the heart."
Hebrews 4:12

What was the most boring event you've ever attended? How long did it actually last compared to how long it felt it lasted? I recall, and I use that word loosely, too many afternoon staff meetings that seemed to be called only to fulfill an arbitrary time requirement. The good news is that I've learned how to almost imperceptibly fall asleep in public.

Boredom is something I really dislike. Not that everything needs to be entertaining but it should capture your attention. You've probably seen boring movies or heard snooze-inducing sermons. Have you ever thought about your classroom? When I first began teaching I was soft-spoken and, well, boring. I would regularly have to awaken students, some of whom had just finished answering a question. I finally realized that not only were the students bored, I was bored as well. To be sure, some of the Math lessons weren't exciting in the least (if you hate Math you're probably trying to figure out if there is ever an exciting Math lesson), but I could've put more energy into them.

Do You See What I See?

One day, through God and the influential exuberance of my colleague Delmás Campbell, I realized a change was needed. That's when I decided to speak with more enthusiasm and walk around the room as I taught. This helped not only with keeping students attentive, but I was now able to see how well they were taking notes and understanding the material. Students were also able to whisper questions as I came around so that they could save themselves from any "embarrassment." Even shy students tended to participate more. The young men, who are always trying to be cool, were engaged. I remember telling one young man who wasn't necessarily known for his academic prowess but should've been, "Mr. Ekeh. I've noticed something. You *like* thinking!" He smiled, acknowledging that I was indeed telling the truth. The energy had become contagious.

Rhoda was a young girl who was involved in a prayer group for Peter. I can imagine that her interests lay elsewhere as this group in the house where she stayed continued to pray for him. She, like the young man who fell out of the window when Paul was preaching, may have fallen asleep during the prayers. When the knock came at the door, however, her energy level increased (young people enjoy movement). She reached maximum excitement when she realized that the one for whom they had been praying had miraculously been freed and was now outside. Her ebullience was so overwhelming that she forgot to open the door!

How wonderful it must have been to move from such an enervating state to an energized one. Not only should our classrooms be that way, but the joy we have about Jesus should be that contagious. Our God is not boring. As His representatives, we shouldn't be either.

Tuesday - Your Challenge and a Teaching Tip

Challenge: This week's challenge is to reread your favorite Bible story and prepare to tell it. You can tell it during class, volunteer to do so for children's story, or help with the youngsters during their lesson study at church. You might even tell the story and make a YouTube video of you doing so. Make sure you tell why this story is important to you. One thing *must* be true - it must capture and keep the attention of your audience. Practice in front of a truth-telling friend if necessary.

Teaching Tip: No matter how large or small your class may be, teach each class as though you're teaching royalty. (You are!) If you're going to teach, do it with all your might. Let the students know they are valued by giving them your best each day. The energy you give is usually reciprocated by them.

Wednesday - Time in the Word

Acts 12:5-17

Thursday - Prayer

Lord, we thank You for giving us life. Even more than that You've given it to us more abundantly. Help us to use every fiber of our being for Your glory, that through our teaching and influence others might be moved to seek You for themselves. As we do so, allow us to simultaneously be daily reinvigorated to follow the path You've laid out for us. It's a privilege to be a worker in Your vineyard. Thank You for the blessing of temporal work with eternal blessings. We pray this all in Jesus' name, amen.

Friday - Reflection

How was your week? Did you complete the challenge? What lessons

Do You See What I See?

did you learn? What did you see God do this week?

_____

_____

_____

_____

_____

_____

Week 37

Cost of Loving

Memory Verse - "So likewise, whoever of you does not forsake all that he has cannot be My disciple."
Luke 14:33

I walked away from $60,000 of free money. I also twice left great teaching jobs to move to a foreign country with no real prospect for work. If you're starting to think I don't like money, you're probably not alone.

Every opportunity has a cost. Whether you're vowing to forsake all others when you get married or regularly giving up part of your weekends to plan lessons and grade papers because you've decided to be a teacher, every opportunity requires us to give up something.

By God's grace, I was granted a $100,000USD fellowship to attend any graduate school of my choice. After being accepted, I was notified that the school matches the fellowship, so the funds from the fellowship came to me. Each semester I was given $10,000. It was a good gig. However, in the midst of my fourth semester, God initiated this conversation with me:

"Are you ready to go?"
"Yes. Where are we going?"
"I'll tell you later. Let's go."

Do You See What I See?

At the end of that semester I left the program with no prospects in sight. Somehow my teaching career began a few months later. I have no regrets.

Eight years later, I left the United States for Jamaica. Five years after that we moved from Jamaica to Australia. When I landed in either place I was unemployed. (Please note that a non-working workaholic can be a miserable person.) Yet God kept me at peace because He was teaching me something both times. The first time was a lesson on how to be a husband, the second on how to be a father. He knew I needed that time to learn and reprioritize, for family is more important than any job.

When I was young I read that it's easier for a camel to go through the eye of a needle than for a rich man to enter into the kingdom of God. I prayed that the Lord wouldn't allow me to get rich. God solved that issue pretty quickly - He told me to be a teacher. The cost of doing what God tells you to do isn't only a behavioral thing, it's a financial thing as well.

Hannah was desperate to have a child. She was willing to pay the cost of looking like a foolish drunk as she prayed publicly for a baby. She knew that there would be the fee of pain in childbirth as a result of Eve's punishment. Yet she was willing to pay more than that - she was prepared to give her child back to the Lord. This was something that would cost her everything, for her worth in society was tied directly to her children. It's one thing to make a deal before the child has arrived. It's another thing altogether not to renege once he's born and you've spent countless waking hours developing his body, mind, and character. But Hannah never wavered. Much like the Father, she was willing to give her son, her everything, for a higher purpose. The cost of living, the cost of loving, would be to give up her life.

What are you willing to give for Jesus? Better yet, what *aren't* you willing to give?

Tuesday - Your Challenge and Teaching Tip

Challenge: The challenge this week will force you to dig deep. It's simple yet may be more arduous for some than others. Sometime in the next 24 hours, give away money to a cause or causes that you deem worthy. Prayerfully decide on an amount that is sacrificial and trust God that He'll use it for His glory. You will be blessed - God guarantees it.

Teaching Tip: Safety must be first, especially with your students. At the cost of being disliked, take the time to be sure that all safety procedures are followed in your classroom and on field trips. Don't cut corners because you, and your school, will be held liable if the procedures in place aren't followed. More than that, being safe and secure is paramount. We must trust God but also do our part.

Wednesday - Time in the Word

1 Samuel 1:9-28

Thursday - Prayer

Lord, I recall the lyrics of an old song that beg the question, *What if I give all*? We are forever indebted to you for Your sacrifice, and what You ask for in return is all of us. The combined goodness of all humanity is worthless compared to what You've given but You accept it anyway because of Christ's blood. Thank You for covering us. Thank You for making us worthy. It's not through our might, power, or by our deeds, but it's by grace through faith that we saved. Grant us Your Spirit, even as demonstrated by the widow giving her two mites, to give all to You. This is our prayer in Jesus' name. Amen.

Friday - Reflection

How was your week? Did you complete the challenge? What lessons did you learn? What did you see God do this week?

_____

_____

_____

_____

_____

_____

_____

Week 38

That Sounds Familial

Memory Verse - "'Be angry, and do not sin'": do not let the sun go down on your wrath."
Ephesians 4:26

Fact: Your family gets on your nerves sometimes.

My sister, Marnel, and I, being one year apart, are very close. As my elder, she's the one who told me that my clothes were horrible looking and I needed to change before we'd leave for middle school. She was also the "enforcer" in our elementary school and she particularly doesn't take kindly to anyone mistreating her family. One time she stood up for me when a boy took my brand new tennis ball and threw it on the roof. I cried. She punched him. We were friends the next day.

Marnel is a professor of communications and has a minor in Mathematics. She called me one day to ask for clarification for a difficult Math question. It ended with her being extremely offended. I don't recall the question but my slowly-stated response, which I admit sounded very sounded patronistic, was

"Because a *negative* times a *negative* is a *positive*."

Of course this is something that children in primary school know. To

151

say it to someone who successfully studied Math on the undergraduate level as if they didn't know it was insulting (especially since she may have taught it to me). My sister was instantly furious.

"Excuse me! Excuse me!! You don't EVER talk to me like that! I have to go.. I have to go!!"
CLICK

We laugh about it often, but to this day she's still slightly (rather, greatly) offended by that conversation.

Has anyone ever spoken to you as if you were inferior? As though you weren't good enough or smart enough? Has anyone ever acted as though your voice didn't matter or taken credit for something that you said or did? It's a terrible experience to go through but it's even worse if it's done by someone close to you. The people who are closest to you, who know you the best, are the ones who can hurt you the most.

Jesus knew this type of pain first-hand when Judas betrayed him with a kiss. This is the same Judas who had worked with Him in ministry, who had helped to feed the 5,000 and performed miracles in His name. The same one whose feet He had just washed. To this Judas, Jesus asked, "*Friend*, why have you come?"

Somehow, despite the betrayal of trust and love, Jesus didn't hold a grudge. Would you do the same?

Tuesday - Your Challenge and a Teaching Tip

Challenge: Contact a family member to whom you haven't spoken in a while. Check on their well-being and, as appropriate, let them know that they are on your prayer list. It's a difficult thing when you're hurt by family, but it's a wonderful thing to know you're loved by them. Share that love today.

Teaching Tip: Having students operate as a caring family teaches great life skills. If done properly, it can also lessen your load. One idea is to assign student-partners who regularly share information and notes with one another. This is especially helpful when students miss lessons. You may have to touch up some loose ends, but this will alleviate the number of times you have to teach and reteach the same lesson.

Wednesday - Time in the Word

Matthew 26:14-25, 47-50

Thursday - Prayer

It's difficult, Lord, when people close to us hurt us, especially since they know more about our pains and trials than others. But You know better than we could how hurtful it can be. It wasn't just Judas, Lord, it was us and the sins we commit today that hurt You deeply. It's those times when we don't do what we know we should and also when we do the things we know we shouldn't that pain You deeply. Forgive us, Lord. Give us the wisdom to know what to do and the strength to do it. Without You we can do nothing good, but with You all things are possible. Lead us, heavenly Father, through the "impossible" times, we ask in Jesus' name. Amen.

Friday - Reflection

How was your week? Did you complete the challenge? What lessons did you learn? What did you see God do this week?

Do You See What I See?

_____

_____

_____

_____

_____

_____

Keeping Down Appearances

Memory Verse - "Abstain from all appearance of evil."
1 Thessalonians 5:22 KJV

Norm..*YOU* can't go there!"

I don't know about you but I don't like being told I *can't* do something. I was about twenty years old when a good friend of mine, Maurice Taffe, said the aforementioned to me. There was a party on the previous Saturday night and I wasn't particularly keen on going but the person taking me home stopped by for a short while. I didn't get out of the car because it wasn't my type of gathering. We left after about 10 minutes.

When I relayed this information to Maurice, his eyes instantly got big. He said to me, in no uncertain terms, that I (a grown man, I thought) was not allowed at that party or any other of that type. I immediately inquired why he gave such a forceful directive.

"Norm, do you know who you are? Do you understand what you represent? If *you* go to a party like that then other people, and their parents, will think it's okay for them to go to that type of party."

I hadn't signed up for it, but it was then that I realized I was a role model. As Jesus says in Luke 12:48, "To whom much is given, much is required."

Years later, a player on a basketball team I coached, Ryan Gordon, told me mid-game that I always needed to keep my cool.

"Coach, if *you* get upset the entire team loses its composure."

Again I realized the weight of leadership. I had to stay calm for my team's sake. There are some little things that have much more of an effect than you would think.

Esther hadn't understood how important her role as queen would be. I imagine she was enjoying the lifestyle that came with the position and, unlike her predecessor, tried to be more diplomatic when dealing with her temperamental and chauvinistic husband. She probably didn't realize how deeply she would soon impact the lives of those around her. As a result of much prayer, fasting, and the reputation she had earned as a loving wife, Esther's appearance before the king was warmly greeted and she was able to save her people from the hand of Haman. Had she made a misstep prior to this moment, it may have cost her and all the Jews in Persia their lives.

Have you considered the fact that your influence can positively or negatively affect the lives of people you've never met? How you carry yourself and respond to criticism, and even where you decide to spend your free time can affect your students, their parents, and countless others. As the school year closes, know that the lives we live speak 1000 times louder than what we say. Speak well. Live better.

Tuesday - Your Challenge and a Teaching Tip

Challenge: Borrowing from the movie *War Room* (2015), make a physical prayer list. It may be on paper or as an electronic spreadsheet. Add to the list as you are led. You may end up like me where there's a different list for each day. Spend quiet time each day praying for these precious souls.

Teaching Tip: In this day and age it is crucial that you are not alone in a private setting with any student without another honest and responsible person nearby, preferably a colleague. It only takes an accusation of impropriety to ruin a reputation and a career. Consider the possible costs and always err on the side of caution.

Wednesday - Time in the Word

Esther 4:5 - 5:3

Thursday - Prayer

Lord, it's difficult to remove our desire for the spotlight. It's nice to be seen and acknowledged, but our goal must be to make You more seen and more acknowledged. As John the Baptist said, we must decrease and You must increase. Show us how to do this so that we might not fall into the traps that have been laid by the enemy since the garden of Eden. Show us how to lift You up so that all men will be drawn to You. Finally, empty us of self so much that Your glory shines through us, that Your appearance in the clouds of glory will be welcomed by us and our loved ones. This is our prayer in the almighty name of Jesus Christ. Amen.

Friday - Reflection

How was your week? Did you complete the challenge? What lessons did you learn? What did you see God do this week?

Do You See What I See?

_____

_____

_____

_____

_____

_____

_____

Week 40

Call Me, I'm There

Memory Verse - "The name of the Lord is a strong tower; The righteous run to it and are safe."
Proverbs 18:10

Hint for Life: Find a rehabilitation center **BEFORE** one is needed.

My dad had had a cardiac arrest and my wife, my one-year-old son, and I had just flown halfway across the world to see him, my mom and my siblings. When we arrived, my dad was making progress, thank God. About a week later he was doing well enough to be moved from the hospital to a rehabilitation center. We were thankful and I booked our return flight. Little did we know the challenge before us.

Have you ever gone to a nursing home/rehab center? If you haven't you should, especially if someone in your family is getting up in age. Many, if not most, are subpar or close to being completely unsuitable. My job on the days before we returned to Australia was to drive around with my mother and find a suitable place for my dad to rehab. My mother has her doctorate in nursing practice and has worked in medicine for over two decades. She knows when a medical facility is a glorified dump.

The hospital recommended a few places for my dad that were near our home. We went online to see the reviews for some and visited others. They were all terrible. All of them. All except one. This was a beautiful and clean facility that we visited where they treated people nicely and communicated with families well. When we returned and told the case worker of our choice she informed us of the simultaneously good and bad news - my dad wasn't sick enough to be sent there. Now, on the day my dad must leave the hospital and the day of our return flight, my father had no place to go.

My mom, aunt, and I hurried to one place that some said would be fine. As we walked out after a short tour my mom wept. It was a dump. We stood in the rainy parking lot with nowhere to turn. I thought to myself, "I wish I knew someone in the rehab business who could pull some strings and get my dad to a proper place." I thought of friends and connections, but no one came to mind who could do something at this late hour. But then I remembered, in the midst of this dark hour, that there was someOne I could call. Yes, we had prayed before, but now was a time like none other. I prayed. We prayed. We all kept praying.

As we drove away, a feeling a peace came over me. God said, "I got it." I wouldn't need to change my flight - I knew God had taken care of it. Shortly thereafter, we got a call from someone who recommended a place close to our home. It was a former hotel building and, after our tour, my mom approved (a minor miracle). I hurriedly rushed home and packed, said goodbye to my family and flew back, knowing that God is, and always will be, in charge...and He's still just a prayer away.

Jesus tells the story of an annoying woman and a wicked man in a position of power. She annoys him to the point that he gives her what she wants because he knows she's not going to stop coming. Jesus, in the book of Matthew, tells us to ask and we shall receive. He doesn't say ask once. We might have to "annoy" Him. We might have to hold onto him and say, like Jacob, that we won't let go until He blesses us. Be certain that, in the midst of these times, God is not only working for you, but working in you. Call Him. I guarantee He'll be there. Because He already is.

Tuesday - Your Challenge and a Teaching Tip

Challenge: I don't like annoying people. They're, for lack of a better word, annoying. It's a pet peeve of mine and my reaction can often not be great to such individuals. The challenge this week is to list the things that get on your nerves - your pet peeves. Then determine whether your reaction to these things is how a Christian should react. If not, make a decided change through the power of God. Get prayerfully ready, as this may change your life.

Teaching Tip: Who you know can indeed be very important, especially years from now. Being known as an excellent educator who is fair and unbiased is the type of reputation you should strive to have. If you ever decide to look elsewhere for work, this can pay great dividends. Earning this distinction requires being consistent everyday. Even if you're a bit disgruntled, don't burn your bridges. Through Christ, all things are possible.

Wednesday - Time in the Word

Luke 18:1-8

Thursday - Prayer

Faith is the victory. Thank You, Lord, for giving each one of us a measure of faith. But, like the father in Mark 9 says, we believe, please help our unbelief. For the stressful times for which we cannot plan ahead,

Do You See What I See?

we ask that You hold us closer to You. In the daily struggles we need Your hand as well. Be our first recourse and our primary resource, that through it all we'll learn to trust You completely. We pray this in the name of the One who is Faithful and True, amen.

Friday - Reflection

How was your week? Did you complete the challenge? What lessons did you learn? What did you see God do this week?

_____

_____

_____

_____

_____

_____

Congratulations!

Congratulations on finishing the school year!

I pray it was a year filled with blessings from God and that you were more fully able to see God's leading in your classroom or office, at your school, and in your life away from work. It is my hope and prayer that this devotional was able to assist you in ministering to His children, even as it ministered to you.

May God continue to use you throughout your future endeavors and may we meet one day in Eternity.

In Jesus' name.

Citations

Bruckheimer, J. & Yakin, B. (2000). *Remember the Titans*. [Motion Picture]. United States: Walt Disney Pictures.

Frank, Natalie. https://www.quora.com/What-is-the-origin-of-the-quote-attributed-to-a-Navy-SEAL-Under-pressure-you-dont-rise-to-the-occasion-you-sink-to-the-level-of-your-training-Where-and-when-was-this-said, 2016.

Westmaas, Reuben. https://curiosity.com/topics/to-get-your-point-across-use-the-serial-positioning-effect-curiosity?utm_campaign=daily-digest&utm_source=sendgrid&utm_medium=email, 2017.

White, Ellen Gould. *The Adventist Home.* Ellen G. White Estate, Inc. 2010.

White, Ellen Gould. *Education*. Ellen G. White Estate, Inc. 2010.

Thanks for Reading

Made in the
USA
Middletown, DE